HOW TO KEEP YOUR COMPANY CULTURE FROM GOING TO SH!T

CHARISSE FONTES

How To Keep Your Company Culture From Going to Shit

A Guide To A Healthy Workplace Culture

Some of the names and identifying details of the individuals in this book have been changed to protect their privacy.

Publication Date: August 17th, 2023

Paperback ISBN: 978-1-7368489-2-0

E-book ISBN: 978-1-7368489-4-4

Published by Charisse Fontes

4425-C Treat Blvd #333

Concord, CA 94521

Visit: culturecircle.co

Email: hello@culturecircle.co

Cover design by Farrukh Khan // @farrukh_bala

For Humanity.

CONTENT

DEAR YOU,

I want to take you beyond the surface of company culture and dive deep into its transformative power. Sprinkled in this book is a story that showcases how company culture can completely alter the course of a person's life, making it one of the most profound elements within any business.

Homeless with two kids and another on the way, I weave in firsthand how a single cultural transformation changed the course of an entire family's life and, in return, empowered thousands of others.

How To Keep Your Culture From Going to Shit is more than just a book—it's a fusion of philosophy, practical tools, and strategies tailored specifically for the workplace and those curious about company culture.

The landscape of humanity is evolving; traditional Human Resource practices are outdated. This exciting shift creates a space where businesses and humanity can coexist, paving the way for the most successful and empowered workforce and economic generation we've ever seen.

Join me on this journey as I dissect company culture from various lenses—through the eyes of humanity, anthropology, spirituality, and practicality. My goal is to provide you with the understanding and empowerment needed to create a healthy and thriving workplace culture.

Bring along your sense of humor and your ever-curious mind. They'll serve you well as we embark on this enlightening adventure together.

With Gratitude,
Charisse

INTRODUCTION

I was homeless with two kids under five and had just found out I was pregnant. Standing at the county office asking for help, I was placed on a shelter waiting list and given vouchers for a few nights at a hotel and then for a motel. Little did I know that this would be the start of a journey that introduced me to the wonderful crafting of company culture.

The shelter had a strict ninety-day limit. At nearly four months pregnant, my goal was to secure a job—scratch that—I needed to secure a job so I could transition into more stable housing somewhere. Without a job, I risked repeating the cycle: giving birth, receiving a few more vouchers, and getting back on the shelter waiting list.

My daily routine consisted of getting up at 7 am, taking a shower, getting my boys ready, and dropping them off at the on-site daycare. Then I completed my chore of cleaning the bathroom that I shared with a family of five. This routine became my normal. Afterward, I would head down to the shelter's computer lab and apply for jobs.

I must have sent out what felt like over 500 job applications. Looking back, all I needed was someone to look past my poorly formatted resume, the typos, and the gaps in my work experience.

And then it happened.

Nobody at work knew I was homeless. I showed up each day, showered and wearing a smile, concealing the fact that I resided in a shelter room with my two young children and shared a bathroom with a family of five.

I couldn't attend any after-work events due to the shelter's curfew. My colleagues didn't know that my clothes came from a pile of donations, sifted through by everyone at the shelter each night. Or the leftovers I brought for lunch were generously provided by local restaurants.

When my team organized a baby shower for me, I spoke into the universe about the baby's nursery I was excited to have, keeping my homelessness a secret. While my manager may have sensed something, she never probed or treated me differently.

Finally, when I secured transitional housing and left the shelter behind, I celebrated silently by treating myself to a dessert from the cafeteria—a small luxury I could now afford.

Throughout it all, nobody in the workplace knew I was homeless.

Despite my challenging circumstances, I excelled in my performance. I was always on time. I showed up as bubbly and friendly. I was known for doing a great job.

This experience taught me a profound lesson: you never know what others might be going through in the workplace.

Of all the investments we make, it's free to be kind.

May this book plant the seeds of humanity in your workplace culture.

May it take the linear parts of business and marry it with the lunar phases of the human.

May your company culture live long and prosper.

May your company culture never go to shit.

CHAPTER 1

THE HISTORY OF THE WORKPLACE

The Industrial Revolution

The workplace's history is a fascinating one. The history I'll share will span between America and Europe, which influenced other countries along the way.

This illustrative example highlights the very essence of the origin of business. Imagine a scenario where I specialize in making pies, and you excel at growing carrots. In the early days, exchanging goods through barter marked the birth of business—a simple yet powerful concept.

However, everything changed with the advent of the Industrial Revolution in the mid-1800s. Sweeping through Europe and America, the movement revolutionized the nature of work. Suddenly, our passion and expertise for pies and carrots found new ways to be harnessed for mass production and profit.

The Industrial Revolution went beyond the realm of pies and carrots; it ushered in an era of mass production, introducing machinery and visionary ideas to meet the evolving demands of a changing market. But amid this progress, a pivotal conflict emerged—the clash between machines and humanity. The rise of factories increased the demand for labor.

Children were ideal employees due to their lower wages, smaller size, and the decreased chances they would organize or protest against harsh working conditions. By the 1900s, approximately 18% of the American workforce comprised individuals under the age of 16.

The influx of immigration to the United States further fueled the supply of labor, including child labor. Families endured mistreatment in the hope that their hard work would secure a better future for generations to come.

Fortunately, reforms addressing child labor emerged in the mid-1900s, gradually integrating children into what we now recognize as the education system. While the topic of education warrants its own exploration, our focus, for now, remains on the intriguing history of the workplace.

I share this historical perspective to underscore how the workplace was initially conceived. Just as the energy and atmosphere during childbirth profoundly impact the birther and the baby, the same holds true for the energy infused into the creation of something.

The energy used to start is often the launching pad and catalyst for anything that follows it.

Only a transcendent experience or force can interrupt this continuous flow, as dictated by the laws of physics and energy.

In essence, the workplace emerged from an energy that failed to honor or acknowledge our shared humanity. The story becomes more complex with the introduction of what we now know as Human Resources (HR), an evolving response to the changing dynamics and challenges faced by the workforce.

By exploring the fascinating journey of the Industrial Revolution and its impact on work, we gain invaluable insights into the foundations of the modern workplace. This historical context sets the stage for delving deeper into the nuances of workplace culture, its evolution, and the strategies that can transform it into a thriving and human-centric environment.

The History of Human Resources

Human Resources first showed up in 1760. The concept of "managing" humans while work was being conducted has been going on for centuries.

If you follow the name changes, they all carry the same energy.

- Industrial Welfare: Late 19th century to early 20th century (1870s-1920s)
- Scientific Management: Late 19th century to early 20th century (1880s-1920s)
- Personnel Management: Early 20th century (1900s)
- Human Resources: Mid-20th century (1940s-1950s)
- Human Capital Management: Late 20th century (1970s)
- Talent Management: Late 20th century to early 21st century (1990s-2000s)
- People Operations: Early 21st century (2000s)
- Employee Experience: Early 21st century (2000s)

Human Resources was created for two main purposes:

1. **To keep workers working**. Businesses felt pressure as the people kept leaving the workplace; without the people, the company would suffer significant losses.

2. **To protect the business** from the people in the workplace unionizing.

"Unions exist because HR has failed the people."

The concept of Human Resources has changed, but still, this underlying stereotype sticks to it like a metallic taste in the mouth, something that businesses can't seem to disassociate from.

HR is often seen as being more focused on protecting and profiting the business rather than prioritizing the needs of the people.

Although HR has contributed to good over the centuries, the changes and progress made are usually reactive solutions rather than proactive ones. It's important to note this because HR has carried the short end of the stick for a while.

Individuals eager to get into HR to help humans find that there is a glass ceiling, an alter-ego they must play. Each decision becomes a trade-off between prioritizing people or profit.

This dichotomy introduces scarcity and fear, which greatly influence workplace culture.

Human Resources needs a new story, starting with "Dear Human" and ending with "Love, Your Humanity Department."

My Non-Traditional Lessons In HR

I didn't follow the traditional path to HR; it just happened. I was number 13 at a fast-growing start-up and overheard someone in Engineering mention sometimes we get paid, and sometimes we don't.

I asked if I could help, and I started taking on a wide range of needed duties that all fell under the HR umbrella.

These are some lessons and thoughts I've had since.

If your people don't trust HR, you have an expensive liability department.

If the culture doesn't feel safe from the people they believe are designed to make them feel safe, they create microcosms. Microcosms in the culture are dangerous because the culture (the people) aren't able to engage, contribute, and do what you've envisioned them to do because they are using up additional energy to maintain survival mode.

Your people need HR they can trust. To know that HR has their back and will speak up for them as they navigate the workplace. Complimentary to that, the culture needs HR to be consistent with the rules of engagement. The minute the culture senses inconsistent patterns (i.e., what HR says it will do vs. what it does). The survival mode is heightened, and things start to shift.

Culture work and HR are two different things.

Too many times in job descriptions, companies ask HR to "own" or "cultivate" the culture. I have fallen into that trap as it seems essential to the work. However, company culture work and HR are two different functions. HR is around maintaining a system, and Culture work is about honoring the variables in and around the system.

To hold both is burnout and disaster waiting to happen because the energy for both are different, and each requires a different frequency to navigate.

Whenever I partner with a company, HR is energetically dehydrated or behind in the people's initiatives and focuses.

This brings me to something else I learned.

Inclusion & Diversity and HR are two different things.

Companies tucking Inclusion or DEI initiatives under HR are destined to fail.

DEI is deeper than most realize, and when you shift these things under HR, you end up with a lukewarm budget and OKRs that go nowhere.

Combining DEI under HR is like combining Marketing and Accounting - they are both functions of revenue and are important, but they carry different energy and a different frequency.

Right now, there are disengaged DEI committees, low budget inclusion initiatives, all leaning towards a place and space that isn't efficient or effective. It's not because people don't care; they do. They followed trends and experts and needed to recognize that this is simpler yet bigger than how it aligns with expectations.

HR needs its own HR.

HR needs its own HR.

HR needs its own HR.

HR needs its own HR.

Going into companies to partner on culture, the HR people are the ones that need the most support as they see and take on everything. They either express their concerns and advocate for themselves, or they stay silent and deal with the "norms" of the job.

While beginning in HR, I had an outside HR service that would be my sounding board, therapist, and advisor. I didn't know some things or felt uncomfortable going to the CEO or Exec team. I needed my own space to process with folks that were unattached and understood.

I'm not a huge fan of commiserating circles, so I needed a different approach than traditional HR groups. I didn't want to be a part of a group where we were all smelling the same shit, and no one knew or forgot what roses were supposed to smell like.

HR done right transcends into a Humanity Department.

I'll share more about this later, but it's time for traditional HR to transcend into Humanity Departments.

Humanity Departments keep all the administrative, legal, and general functions of HR; however, the department's philosophy is rooted and foundationally grounded in humanity.

This might seem like a mix between kumbaya and kombucha - but think about it this way. Every person, regardless of their gender, ethnicity, how they identify, background, upbringing, or any other label society has given, wants to be treated like a human and with humanity.

Begin Here

Recap

- The Industrial Revolution, which took place in the mid-1800s, revolutionized the nature of work. It brought about mass production, the introduction of machinery, and innovative visions to meet the evolving market demands.
- The rise of factories during the Industrial Revolution created a surge in demand for workers, leading to the employment of children due to their lower wages and perceived advantages in size and compliance with working conditions.

- Immigration to the United States further fueled the supply of labor, including child labor, as families endured mistreatment in the hope of securing a better future for future generations.
- Reforms addressing child labor emerged in the mid-1900s, integrating children into the education system and improving working conditions.
- Human Resources (HR) emerged as a response to the need for managing human capital and addressing workforce challenges. Initially, HR focused on mitigating worker turnover and preventing employee unionization.
- Over time, HR has evolved and undergone name changes. However, there is a persistent stereotype that HR prioritizes protecting and profiting the business over serving the people.

Reflective Question

How has the historical evolution of the workplace and HR impacted how we perceive work, the treatment of employees, and the relationship between business and people in modern organizations?

Action

Assess your organization's HR practices and workplace culture. Identify areas where historical paradigms may still be influencing decision-making, and explore ways to shift towards a more human-centric and inclusive approach.

Commander Data: The interpretation of visions and other metaphysical experiences are almost always culturally derived, and I have no culture of my own.

Captain Jean-Luc Picard: Yes, you do. You're a culture of one, which is no less valid than a culture of one billion.

– A Conversation From Star Trek: The Next Generation

CHAPTER 2

CULTURE 101

Understanding the history of the workplace, including the Industrial Revolution and the evolution of HR, is crucial for laying the foundation of the conversation around culture.

When you search for the definition of company culture, you may come across a range of interpretations.

To provide a grounded perspective, I offer a definition inspired by my background as an anthropologist and philosopher:

Company Culture
/ˈkəmp(ə)nē/ /ˈkəlCHər/

An evolving survival mechanism encompassing thoughts, beliefs, actions, and responses that people use to achieve mutually satisfying goals within the workplace.

The key aspect of this definition is the recognition of culture as an evolving survival mechanism. This implies that culture's primary concern is to adapt and thrive within its environment, making it a vital component of organizational success.

Most company cultures are on the defensive, identifying threats, detecting broken patterns, and striving to stay one step ahead of what lies ahead. However, the ideal state for a culture is to be on the offense, proactive, creative, efficient, and rapidly improving.

As we go deeper into this book, one goal is to inspire your culture to adopt a more proactive approach, where the true magic happens.

I often see the parallels between the definition of company culture and our daily lives. Many individuals navigate their lives through three categories: survival, success, and significance.

Survival represents our basic needs—what is necessary for sustenance. It often follows a pattern of daily awareness or consciousness. For instance, observing a squirrel hoarding food, we witness their daily awareness in action, accumulating as much as they can, even if they already have enough.

Success is where most people aspire to be, as it is the next level that goes beyond daily awareness. However, success can be relative, varying from person to person. While society attempts to define universal success, many have pursued societal expectations only to find emptiness in the end.

Significance is the ultimate goal we seek throughout our lives—to have a sense of purpose and meaning, knowing that our actions and existence hold significance beyond the superficial. We yearn to make a positive impact that extends far beyond ourselves.

You may be wondering how all of this connects to company culture and its relevance. The answer lies in understanding that your company culture, as an evolving survival mechanism, is intricately linked to the pursuit of significance.

However, there is a fourth layer that many of us seek intuitively: transcendence. Being in the space of transcendence means that regardless of whether we are in survival, success, or significance, our actions and impact extend beyond ourselves, positively influencing those we may never even meet.

At Culture Circle, the boutique culture partner company I run, we embrace the notion of being "the roots to the tree, of which we'll never experience the shade." Our purpose and focus evolve beyond the pursuit of growth and profit to serve as the foundational elements—seed, soil, water, and roots—for humanity and the workplace.

Understanding all these aspects becomes relevant for comprehending that your company culture is an evolving survival mechanism. By recognizing the trajectory towards significance, you can amplify the impact of your culture.

To truly understand workplace culture, it is essential to realize that your people embody the collective sum of your company culture. Observe the phases and stages your culture undergoes, as they provide patterns and clues you can use to communicate effectively with your culture, regardless of the season.

By refining your understanding of culture and its connection to human experiences, you will be better equipped to shape and nurture a thriving and meaningful company culture.

What Your Company Culture Wants

There are universal culture laws that transcend regardless of the industry, size, or core purpose of the business, making it both easy and complex to track.

I'll walk you through these laws and the ways to think about them. In the end, I've provided some reflective space and questions to think about as they relate to the current state of your company culture.

Let's dive in.

#1: The Law of Safety

Creating a safe environment for your culture is key. When your culture feels safe, the people can relax, exist, and flourish. By minimizing perceived threats and providing a sense of security, your culture can focus its energy on growth and productivity.

As we discussed earlier, there is a correlation between survival, success, and significance in both the human experience and the business realm. It is important to recognize that most individuals live their lives navigating survival and success, making safety a significant aspect.

Your culture will naturally shift between survival and success, especially during the early and rapid growth phases. The key factor in each of these stages is the need for your culture to feel safe.

By reducing the need to be constantly alert, your culture can redirect its energy toward achieving success and significance. This, in turn, promotes efficiency, creativity, critical thinking, and innovation.

When we perceive a threat, our bodies release stress hormones like cortisol and activate the sympathetic nervous system, triggering the fight-or-flight response. These physiological changes are meant to prepare us for immediate action to ensure survival.

However, in this defensive state, the brain prioritizes immediate physical protection over higher-level cognitive functions like creative thinking. The resources and attention of the brain are redirected toward addressing the perceived threat, which can hinder our ability to engage in innovative and creative problem-solving.

Cultivating a safe environment and minimizing perceived threats is important for allowing individuals to access their full cognitive capabilities, fostering a conducive atmosphere for creativity and innovation to thrive.

So, what does this mean for you?

It means that safety should be a strategic consideration if you want to ensure that your culture moves beyond mere survival and enters a space of growth and mutual benefit. By intentionally cultivating a safe environment, you empower your culture to thrive, leading to increased productivity and the realization of its full potential.

#2 The Law of Value

Your culture wants to know it has meaning, worth, and value. This extends beyond individualistic notions of value and focuses on the collective of your culture. Ultimately, the culture wants to understand that its actions are meaningful and that their significance is tied to a deeper purpose.

Our humanity is evolving and starting to shift away from the prescribed linear expectations imposed by society. People are increasingly drawn to finding what truly ignites their passion and living in alignment with their inner being rather than conforming to external expectations.

Consider the example of someone who pursued a path solely to make their parents proud, investing years of education and effort to achieve outstanding academic success. Yet, they ultimately decide to leave a high-paying career, move to Costa Rica, and dedicate themselves to preserving wildlife and nature on a compound. This demonstrates the call towards something greater, the pull towards a meaningful existence that resonates with our inner selves.

We are collectively experiencing a longing for more, a yearning for a deeper sense of purpose. Consequently, we can also sense when that purpose is absent or lacking.

One of your goals as a leader is to ensure that your culture has a collective understanding of its value, meaning, and worth within a larger ecosystem. By providing opportunities for your culture to explore and embrace the significance of their work, you can ignite a powerful shift that has the potential to move mountains.

Consider incorporating tools and avenues that allow your culture to connect with the larger purpose and impact of their work. Whether through storytelling, shared experiences, or aligning with a meaningful mission, you can empower your culture to recognize its integral role in creating a positive impact.

#3 The Law of Confidence

The law of confidence highlights the importance of reassured confidence along the journey of your company culture. Similar to emotional commitment, which we will explore later in this book, confidence ebbs and flows throughout the culture's evolution.

The key aspect of this law is that when your culture seeks confidence, it must find it, regardless of the situation. Confidence becomes a significant milestone that can make or break crucial moments.

Your culture acknowledges that "shit is going to happen," but the primary focus is not on the occurrence of problems themselves. What truly matters is the assurance that things will be okay and that solutions are consistently sought after.

"Okay" refers to any action that doesn't trigger a defensive or protective response within the culture. It implies that your people can rely on decisions being made in their best interest as well as the business. Striking a balance is essential. When decisions are inadequately explained or perceived to prioritize the business over the well-being of the people, the culture becomes susceptible to questioning, doubt, and the emergence of alternative narratives.

These factors can undermine the confidence needed for the culture to coexist and co-create with the core objectives of the company.

Begin Here

Recap:

- The basics of company culture include understanding its definition and the history of the workplace.
- Company culture is an evolving survival mechanism that encompasses thoughts, beliefs, actions, and responses within the workplace.
- There is a correlation between survival, success, and significance in both human experience and business, making safety a significant aspect.
- Culture seeks safety to relax, exist, and flourish, enabling focus on growth and productivity.
- Providing a safe environment minimizes perceived threats and fosters a conducive atmosphere for creativity and innovation.
- Culture wants to know if its work has meaning, worth, and value tied to a deeper purpose.
- Aligning work with personal values and a sense of purpose promotes a more fulfilling and engaged culture.

- Confidence is crucial for culture, assuring that challenges are met with solutions and that things will be okay.
- Balancing decisions that benefit both the people and the business builds confidence within the culture.

Reflective Question:

How can you create a culture that prioritizes safety, meaning, and confidence to empower individuals and foster growth?

Action

Assess your current culture and identify areas for improvement. Implement measures to enhance safety, such as transparent communication and feedback channels. Provide opportunities for employees to connect with the deeper purpose and impact of their work. Foster a culture of confidence by ensuring decisions are explained and perceived as fair and beneficial to both the people and the business.

We have explored the concept of company culture and its desires. In the upcoming chapter, we will shift our perspective and examine something that many companies have, and even more people fall for them, yet what I am about to share the culture does not want it, and it fails to serve the best interests of both the people and the company. I'm talking about Deep Fake Perks.

Appearance is not always reality; what appears to be real may, in fact, be an illusion."

- Plato

CHAPTER 3

DEEP FAKE PERKS

Deep Fake Perks (DFP) are enticing benefits and perks offered by companies to attract and retain employees. These perks may include trendy office spaces, recreational facilities, unlimited vacation policies, free meals, game rooms, or social events. They create the illusion of an ideal work environment and a caring company culture. However, over time, the deceptive nature of Deep Fake Perks becomes apparent.

After the initial excitement wears off, employees may find that these perks are superficial and fail to address the underlying issues they face in their work and personal lives. They may end up working longer hours, sacrificing personal time, and feeling overwhelmed by high expectations and constant connectivity. For instance, a company might boast about flexible working hours or unlimited vacation but neglect to address excessive or inefficient meetings, resulting in a work environment where time off feels guilt-inducing or leads to a heavier workload upon return.

Deep Fake Perks can be detrimental to employees' well-being and work-life balance. They create a false sense of support and fulfillment while diverting attention from more significant issues such as excessive workload, poor management practices, or a lack of meaningful engagement and growth opportunities. Recognizing these perks is crucial because 80% of chronic diseases are caused by a lack of boundaries in lifestyle.

The truth is, Deep Fake Perks don't truly serve employees or the company. They are designed to keep employees hooked, investing counterintuitively in instant gratification and perception, all while the company quietly whispers, "Forget about your personal life; we've got everything you need right here!"

Both employees and companies need to recognize the true nature of Deep Fake Perks. Employees should identify when perks are merely cosmetic and evaluate if they genuinely contribute to their well-being and professional development. Companies, on the other hand, should reassess their approach to perks and benefits, prioritizing authentic support, a healthy work environment, and addressing the real needs of their employees.

By breaking free from Deep Fake Perks, employees can prioritize their well-being and career growth, while companies can create a more genuine and fulfilling work culture that supports their employees' success.

How to Break Away from Deep Fake Perks: Understand Your Demographic

To break away from the cycle of Deep Fake Perks and design benefits and perks that truly support your employees, it's essential to understand your company's demographic. Avoid the copy and paste or copycat perks that seem like a great idea, yet either are counter-intuitive to the company culture or don't make sense for the type of demographics you have in the workplace.

Take a closer look at the makeup of your workforce and consider where your employees are in their lives. Are you a multi-generational workplace? If so, what matters most to each person? Identify the themes or categories that emerge from this understanding and tailor your perks accordingly.

For example, if a significant portion of your workforce is interested in achieving financial freedom or purchasing real estate, consider offering perks that support these goals. It could be financial planning workshops, educational resources on investing, or even assistance with down payments for housing.

Deep Fake Perks exist because they were never designed to genuinely help employees. While there may be some benefits, their primary purpose is to keep people content while focusing on comfort, convenience, and conformity.

Make it a practice to regularly assess your demographic's needs. Consider an annual review for significant aspects like healthcare renewal and evaluate every 3-6 months for more flexible perks. Treat each initiative as a pilot, an experiment aimed at creating meaningful experiences for your employees. By doing so, you'll be on the right path to providing authentic support and fostering a culture that truly benefits your workforce.

Begin Here

Recap:

- Deep Fake Perks are enticing benefits that may appear attractive but fail to deliver sustainable value or support to employees.
- These perks create an illusion of an ideal work environment and company culture but often neglect to address underlying issues.
- Employees may find themselves working longer hours, sacrificing personal time, and feeling overwhelmed despite the presence of these perks.
- Deep Fake Perks can be detrimental to well-being and work-life balance, diverting attention from more significant issues.
- Recognizing the true nature of Deep Fake Perks is crucial for both employees and companies.

- Employees should evaluate whether perks genuinely contribute to their well-being and professional development.
- Companies should reassess their approach to perks, focusing on authentic support and addressing real employee needs.

Reflective Question

Are there any perks or benefits in your current workplace that may be considered "Deep Fake Perks"? How do they impact your well-being and work-life balance?

Action

Take the time to understand the demographic makeup of your company's workforce and identify your employees' specific needs and priorities. Tailor perks and benefits to address these needs authentically and provide genuine support for your workforce's success and well-being. Regularly assess and review these initiatives to ensure they continue to meet the evolving needs of your employees. Treat each initiative as an experiment to create meaningful experiences for your workforce, fostering a culture that genuinely benefits them.

In the eyes of the beginner, there are millions of options.
In the eyes of the expert, there are one or two.

– Shunryu Suzuki

A Story About a Fictional Character Named Birdsnest

Long ago in China, there lived a monk who perched on a certain tree every day to meditate.

No matter if the tree swayed in fierce winds and rain, the monk settled himself comfortably, high up in the branches. Because of this, he was nicknamed "Birdsnest" by the village folk nearby.

Many of these villagers passed beneath the monk while hunting or while gathering wood in the forest, and after a time, they grew used to him. Some began to stop and talk of their concerns with Birdsnest.

They liked the things he had to say, and soon Birdsnest become known for his kind and thoughtful words.

After some years, the monk's wise reputation spread throughout the province. Visitors from distant cities hiked to the remote forest for advice.

Even the Governor of the Provence decided that he, too, would like to visit Birdsnest to discuss matters of importance.

So, one spring morning, the Governor set off to find him. After traveling for several days, he at last located Birdsnest's tree in the dense forest.

The monk sat calmly, high in the topmost branches, enjoying the warmth and the birdsong of spring.

Looking up, the Governor shouted, "Birdsnest! I am the Governor of this Provence, and I have come a great distance to speak with you! I have a most important question!" The Governor waited for a reply but heard only the pleasant sounds of leaves stirring in the breeze.

The Governor continued, "This is my question: tell me, Birdsnest, what is it that all the wise ones have taught? Can you tell me the most important thing the Buddha ever said?"

There was a long pause – just the soft rustle of leaves again.

Finally, the monk called down from the tree: "This is your answer, Governor: Don't do bad things. Always do good things. That's what the Buddha's taught."

But the Governor thought this answer far too simple to have walked two days for! Irritated and annoyed, he stammered, "Don't do bad things; always do good things! I knew that when I was three years old, monk!"

Looking down at the Governor, Birdsnest replied with a wry smile, "Yes, the 3-year-old knows it, but the 80-year-old still finds it difficult to do!"

As we transition to the core of this book, I wanted to share the story of Birdsnest with you. Like the Governor in the story, one might perceive what I'm about to share as simple, common knowledge—the basics.

However, it's important to recognize that many company cultures struggle with simplicity, and toxic workplaces are an all-too-familiar experience for most of us. We often forget the fundamental whispers of wisdom that, if applied, have the power to transform not only us as leaders and culture facilitators but also everyone who comes into contact with it.

CHAPTER 4

HIRE LIKE YOU GIVE A SHIT

After experiencing five failed job interviews, I came to realize that being four-and-a-half months pregnant and potentially needing accommodations, along with upcoming maternity leave, didn't make me the ideal candidate—even though I could do the job. But everything changed when I was contacted by a head recruiter at a one of the Bay Area's leading recruiting firms. It felt like all my momentum had led to this moment.

When I met Sara, there was an instant connection. I went through two hiring processes—one with the recruiting firm and another with South San Francisco's leading Biotech Company.

On the day of the interview, I wore donated clothes I had found the night before in the shelter's donation bin. I was nervous and needed this to go well. We needed this to go well.

As I walked into the pristine lobby, my nerves were amplified. But then I was greeted by Marceline, the receptionist, whose warm and friendly face immediately put me at ease. She had a guest badge ready for me, and we chatted happily, like old friends both excited to see each other.

Ding.

The elevator arrived, and the main Executive Assistance for one of the Directors in the department I was interviewing for came out to greet me. Her friendliness and the fact that she was also pregnant made me smile. While we were in the elevator together, she made a comment, gently grabbing her belly, that her baby was actively moving. My smile widened, she couldn't tell but my little one was doing the same. It was as if our babies were communicating with each other.

In the interview room, I found water and a few snacks waiting for me. I met with four individuals from the department whom I would potentially support. With each smile and kind conversation, my nerves gradually subsided.

And then, I encountered the woman who would change my life forever.

Valerie, my manager.

Am I talent, or am I talented?

- Charisse Fontes

The Current State of Hiring

Currently, companies are striving to recruit top talent, foster inclusivity, and embrace the diverse range of individuals within their environments. Achieving this goal requires implementing an exceptional hiring methodology and process.

In today's landscape of remote, hybrid, and in-office work dynamics, the ability to hire and work from anywhere has revolutionized the game. Moreover, with the growing emphasis on work-life balance, companies must discard antiquated and outdated hiring practices.

One aspect that needs reconsideration is the concept of 'Culture Fit'; it is the archenemy of a healthy company culture.

Clothes are meant to fit.
Shoes are meant to fit.
Gloves are meant to fit.
Rings are meant to fit.
Hats are meant to fit.
People are designed to belong*.

*a sense of inclusion and embraced identity within a community or group of people.

Culture Fit Is Myth

Culture "Fit" is a myth.

Created by corporate, adopted by startups.

Culture Fit indicates a pre-determined box that you want someone to form and assimilate into

By design, it's exclusive.

Folks that use Culture Fit don't understand the culture.

Culture is continuously evolving.

What fits now won't fit later.

Culture "Add" invests in the culture's evolution and company success and empowers the human.

Culture Add

If you look up the recipe for a toxic workplace, you'll find that Culture Fit is one of the ingredients. However, the antidote to this toxic element is Culture Add.

Placing excessive emphasis on Culture Fit can have detrimental and sometimes irreversible effects on your company culture. It is crucial to approach this aspect of the hiring process with intention and thoughtfulness.

While candidates may be rejected based on their fit, it is equally important to invest time and effort into evaluating the value they can add to your company. Recognizing that company culture is an ever-evolving survival mechanism that drives people towards a shared goal is essential.

When onboarding new hires, it is important to ensure that they can contribute to the direction and culture of your company. In one of my VP roles I partnership with The Posse Foundation, an organization that guided young individuals, whom they referred to as scholars from diverse backgrounds and paired them with companies in leadership or decision-making roles.

What resonated with me was their definition of leadership. They acknowledged that some of their scholars had taken care of or even raised their younger siblings, and had demonstrated leadership skills and experience that translated into the workplace. This experience-based approach to leadership struck a chord with me, as life is our most powerful teacher.

A well-designed workplace embraces both traditionally trained leaders and those who have gained valuable lessons through real-life experiences.

This is the essence of Culture Add.

Now, where do company values come into play with all of this?

It's important to acknowledge that company values and company culture are two different things.

You can technically run a company without establishing, announcing, or throwing values on the wall.

You can't run a company without culture.

So, when you hire, look at each person you bring in as adding to your culture. Ideally, you want them to add something great and expansive. However, there are times when that isn't always the case. Someone you might bring in could add something that causes friction and challenges to the culture.

Embracing Culture Add

Culture add involves being mindful and intentional at every stage of the hiring process. It means meticulously crafting ways to identify individuals who not only align with the job requirements but also bring something valuable to the existing culture.

To achieve this, you must first determine what these individuals will add to your company. Clarity and vision are essential in this regard.

Avoid seeking Culture Fit, as doing so can hinder growth and empowerment by promoting conformity.

By fully embracing Culture Add and making it a priority in your hiring decisions, you can foster a vibrant and diverse work environment. This approach enables your company to thrive and excel, benefiting from the unique contributions of exceptional individuals.

Here's how to do it.

Begin with the End

When designing a hiring process, it's essential to have a clear understanding of the desired outcome. If your goal is to hire the best person who will make a positive addition to both the company and its culture, this section is for you.

Let's start by focusing on the company culture. It's great to align your hiring with the idea of Culture Add, but it's even better if you can pinpoint specific aspects of the culture you'd like the new hire to enhance or amplify.

For example, if your company culture embraces the art of efficiency, you'd want to approach hiring with that lens in mind. Look for candidates who can contribute to the existing efficiency or amplify it, even if they may not be experts at being efficient.

Next, consider the vision for your company in the next three to five years (or 18-28 months for smaller companies). Taking the time to envision the future will help you identify areas that are already covered and those that need attention to achieve your goals.

Once you have a clear understanding of what will be an "add" to both the company from a functional and culture perspective, design a job description with intention and purpose. This is the most effective way to attract exceptional individuals who align with your company's values and objectives.

By starting with a well-defined end goal, you streamline your hiring process, prioritize essential criteria, and make more informed decisions. Embracing this approach increases your chances of finding and attracting great people who will contribute to the success and growth of your organization.

Balance the Bias

Our brains are wired for bias. It's how we categorize information. Where it gets tricky is when we consume information that causes conflict between the purpose of the bias and how we treat others.

In a workshop I teach called Understanding Bias for Foundational Inclusion, I explain that our brains are divided into two systems.

System 1 and System 2.

System 1 is fast, automatic, intuitive, and emotional process. It generates impressions and judgments quickly, without requiring conscious effort or verbalization. It relies on associations and patterns learned through repeated

System 2 thinking is slower, conscious, and effortful process. It involves deliberate reasoning, logical analysis, and complex computations. It requires conscious attention and can be used for critical thinking.

While like to think we can operate both at the same time the truth is the two systems conflict with each other.

A product of this type of conflict result in the rational that we can text and drive based on the singular thought of we can text with ease and we know how to drive, so texting and driving together must make sense. However that type of behavior and pattern of thinking never accounts for the variables on the road.

As I delved into anthropological and scientific perspectives, I discovered more about bias, both in my own life and as it relates to hiring.

Acknowledging bias in the hiring process is vital, whether it's conscious or unconscious. We all have biases and denying their existence can lead to more significant problems beyond hiring decisions. Understanding your biases is an ongoing journey, not a destination, and remember that having biases doesn't make you a bad person.

In some cases, biases can be uncomfortable or embarrassing. However, the key lies in how we act upon them. The core purpose of a bias comes from our brain's tendency to categorize new people and new information. To learn quickly, the brain connects new people or ideas to past experiences. Once the new thing has been put into a category, the brain responds to it the same way it does to other things in that category. That creates our biases.

Biases serve to save our brain energy and make decision-making more efficient. The challenge with biases today is that we are exposed to an overwhelming amount of information that can either reinforce or challenge our biases.

As you venture into hiring within your company, I encourage you to work on balancing biases. One way to achieve this is by recognizing when a bias arises from an overused stereotype and shifting from close-ended statements to open-ended questions. For example:

Close-ended statement: "Everyone from that part of town is uneducated."

Open-ended question: "Is everyone from that part of town uneducated?"

Additionally, consider naming your biases. I named mine Bianca. Naming your biases allows you to engage with them consciously. You can then inquire within yourself where these biases originate and question their validity.

The process of naming biases empowers you to tame them and achieve a better balance, allowing the best parts of your humanity to guide your hiring decisions. By actively working to mitigate biases, you create a balanced and more inclusive hiring process that benefits both your company and the candidates you consider.

Hack the Hiring

I've hired over 250 people in my career, and I'm excited to share my all-time best hiring hack with you.

Imagine you've put a lot of thought and effort into crafting a job description, and you've just posted it on various job-seeking platforms like Linkedin, Indeed, and Monster. As expected, your inbox or ATS is now flooded with applicants.

However, the challenge arises when you realize you can't possibly interview or get back to every candidate. Sorting through everyone's applications and resumes becomes a daunting task.

Here's where my hiring hack comes in:

At the bottom or top of the resume (I prefer both), list three simple actions that are required for each application.

For example, when I was hiring for an Office Manager, I asked each applicant to:

1. Send their resume to a specific email address that I had designated for hiring with the subject: 'First & Last Name, Office Manager'.
2. Share a book or movie that resonated with them.
3. Solve a riddle or answer a question.

This ingenious hack not only saved me time by filtering out candidates who didn't follow the instructions, but it also allowed each person to showcase their uniqueness and personality, opening the door to more engaging conversations during the interviews.

By choosing actions that wouldn't take up much of their time, I received enjoyable responses that shed more light on the candidates' qualities and capabilities.

Implementing this hack in your hiring process can lead to more efficient and meaningful interactions, making the whole process a rewarding experience for both you and your candidates.

Conversation vs. Interrogation

Every interview you conduct is valuable time spent, provided it fosters a genuine conversation. Approach each interaction without rigid conditions, simply aiming to engage in a constructive discussion that helps identify the next Culture Add within your company.

Shifting the dynamic from interrogation to conversation alleviates pressure on both the interviewer and the interviewee, creating a comfortable and engaging experience.

To achieve this, two key aspects come into play: asking the right questions and establishing clear decision-making factors.

Over time, interview questions have evolved, moving away from generic ones like "tell me about yourself" to more insightful queries that delve into the candidate's experiences and essence as a person. For instance, instead of asking, "tell me about yourself," ask about a significant highlight that includes one personal and one professional accomplishment. During the sharing of both they will share more about themselves and it will flow more naturally.

Asking intelligent, conversational questions about the person's background and character provides a more comprehensive understanding of the candidate.

If you find yourself reading off the person's resume during the interview, it won't be a great interview experience.

Returning to intention, when seeking a new hire, what will your decision be based on?

Defining this beforehand helps keep biases and egos in check, especially when multiple stakeholders are involved in the decision-making process.

To level the playing field and align expectations for all candidates, it's essential to establish clear deciding factors. By choosing five to seven relevant criteria, you can consistently evaluate candidates on key aspects.

Here are some examples to consider:

1. Availability: Determine the ideal timing that aligns with your company's needs. For instance, if a candidate cannot start within the next month, consider how this factor weighs in the overall decision.

2. Type of Experience: Define whether you prefer candidates with more formal or informal experience. Assess whether you value traditional or non-traditional backgrounds.

3. Years of Experience: Decide the significance of a candidate's experience level. Does it matter more if someone has been doing the job for 3 years or 8 years?

4. Salary Expectations: Address salary expectations early in the process. If a candidate's range exceeds the role's budget, consider whether it's worth having a conversation about it or if you should move on to other candidates.

5. Ability to Demonstrate Top Skills: Clearly outline your top three must-have skills required for the job. During interviews, assess whether candidates can showcase these skills effectively.

Having these deciding factors in place ensures that your interviews are conducted with fairness and consistency. It also facilitates more focused conversations and makes the overall hiring process more efficient and effective.

Go Beyond

Designing your hiring process should be simple, flexible, and infused with elements of fun.

One effective approach is to consider all the human touch points that thread from the initial "Hello," the first moment of contact, to the final "Hire," the last touchpoint before their first day.

Be mindful of avoiding the temptation to copy and paste hiring practices from other companies. Each organization has its unique culture and requirements, so design your process with your company's specific needs in mind.

Hiring is an integral part of business that will never go away. It's crucial for businesses to continuously seek out exceptional individuals to help them achieve greatness.

However, one of the challenges with hiring is that it often becomes personal quickly, which contradicts the professional and business-oriented approach. You must find a balance between connecting with candidates on a human level and making objective hiring decisions.

As humans, there isn't a linear way to conduct the hiring process; however, having clear moral principles around your hiring practices is of utmost importance. Morals differ from rules, which are bound by guidelines and laws with consequences if not followed. Morals, on the other hand, come from within us and guide us in making humane and ethical decisions throughout the hiring journey.

If the recruiter that found me had followed the rules over her moral compass, you wouldn't be reading this book, and my story would look very different.

As you embark on your hiring journey within your company, remember the profound opportunity you have to change the world through each interview, call back, or redirection email. My hope is that you start to challenge the "norms" when it comes to hiring, recognizing that extraordinary approaches can transcend conventional practices and lead to transformative outcomes.

Begin Here

Recap:

- The current state of hiring requires a shift towards fostering inclusivity and embracing diversity in the workplace.
- "Culture Add" is as an alternative to the traditional "Culture Fit," emphasizing the value of candidates who can contribute positively to the company culture.
- Be mindful of bias in the hiring process and reflect on practical steps to balance biases.
- Include simple actions in job applications to filter candidates and create engaging interactions during interviews.
- Shift the interview dynamics from interrogation to conversation by focusing on asking insightful and conversational questions to better understand candidates.
- Establish clear decision-making factors in the hiring process to ensure consistency and fairness when evaluating candidates.

- Focus on human touch points, flexibility, and fun while avoiding copying practices from other companies.
- Have clear moral principles in hiring practices to create a humane and ethical hiring journey that values individuals beyond just their skills and qualifications.

Reflective Question

How can I shift my hiring approach from focusing solely on "Culture Fit" to embracing the concept of "Culture Add" and valuing the unique contributions that candidates can bring to our company culture?

Action

Revisit the hiring lens with a focus on "Culture Add" instead of "Culture Fit." Use this perspective to shape job postings and interview questions. Identify and address biases that might contribute to the counterintuitive nature of culture fit. Keep it simple and concise for a more inclusive and diverse hiring approach.

"We are made for goodness. We are made for love...We are made for all of the beautiful things that you and I know. We are made to tell the world that there are no outsiders...all are welcome."

Demond Tutu

CHAPTER 5

WELCOME LIKE YOU GIVE A SHIT

I was just finishing up my morning chore at the shelter when my phone rang. Cleaning a shared bathroom with a family of five wasn't the most enjoyable chore, but being five months pregnant, it was one of the least physically demanding, so I was grateful for that. I found some solace in doing the cleaning.

The call was from Sarah, and she had some exciting news to share. One of the top biotech companies in the country wanted to hire me on a 12-month contract! The pay was good enough for me to consider moving into transitional housing.

Transitional housing is dedicated to people and families in that in-between phase of housing. You have a job, things are coming together, but you just need some transition time to ensure everything stays consistent, so when you do get permanent housing, you can keep and maintain it.

I was thrilled about the job offer, but at the same time, I had an "oh shit" moment. I realized I hadn't told Sarah or my soon-to-be employer about my pregnancy.

Despite the initial panic, I completed all the necessary paperwork and confirmed my start date.

On my first day, I felt a mix of excitement and conflict. I decided to wait until the third day to share my news with my manager.

Seeing Marceline again was such a breath of fresh air. Her familiar face and energy were just as excited as mine. This time, instead of a guest badge, I proudly wore an official badge.

Valerie, my manager, came to greet me at the lobby. There was something special about her, even from the interview. Her heart and demeanor were kind and welcoming. As the director of the department I was supporting, she was very involved and hands-on.

My desk was thoughtfully set up right outside her office, organized by the other admins in the department.

I was taken around the floor, introduced to the other admins, and shown the copy machines, supply closet, maternity rooms, and the cafeteria, which would soon become a milestone for me.

My first day was a highlight, giving me a glimpse of what to expect. Despite all the personal challenges I was going through, feeling welcomed in the workplace made me feel more human and hopeful for the future.

There are two days you'll never be able to do over.

The first and the last.

Welcoming Is Cultural

Welcoming is cultural. In Tibet, monks would stick out their tongues to show that they came in peace—and weren't the reincarnation of a cruel 9th-century king named Lang Darma, known for having a black tongue. Needless to say, the greeting caught on.

The Māori people of New Zealand have their way of welcoming with the hongi. They press together their foreheads and noses in what is called a "sharing of breath." This greeting signifies the sacred welcoming of a visitor into Māori culture and is used at pōwhiri (Māori welcoming ceremonies)—although the honor requires an invitation and isn't extended to everyone.

In Zimbabwe, the clapping of hands comes after folks shake hands in a call and answer style—the first person claps once, and the second person claps twice in response. Just be careful how you slap those palms together; men clap with fingers and palms aligned, and women with their hands at an angle. In northern Mozambique, people also clap, but three times before they say "moni" (hello).

No matter how much you know about your culture, your culture has a way of welcoming each other.

The Impact of Welcoming

Welcoming is a universal thing and something the workplace culture could do better at, given that the entry or origin beginning of each person you bring on is tied to their overall experience and how long they will be at your company.

Welcoming someone into your culture starts long before their actual arrival. There's a certain energy that goes into the experience, and it can be palpable.

Your new hire can immediately sense whether their desk was hastily thrown together or if someone took the time to set it up thoughtfully.

For me, one of the most rewarding aspects of People and Culture roles was crafting five-star onboarding experiences. I meticulously designed a flow that made the entire onboarding journey meaningful and unforgettable.

That's when I came up with what I now call "Hello-to-Hire." This approach captures the essence of our welcoming process, ensuring that every new hire feels valued and embraced from the very beginning.

Hello-to-Hire, Inspire, & Retire

It's a journey that starts from the moment you post the job description and continues until the moment they bid farewell. Taking a strategic and holistic approach to this process ensures that along every step of the way, your new hires feel valued, supported, and inspired.

The journey is divided into three key phases: HELLO-to-HIRE, INSPIRE, and RETIRE.

HELLO-to-HIRE covers everything from the initial job posting to the new hire's first day. It highlights the need for a well-thought-out and seamless onboarding experience that starts from the moment the role is created. Attention to detail matters, as simple gestures like thoughtfully setting up their desk can make a significant difference in how they feel welcomed.

The next phase, INSPIRE, focuses on onboarding beyond the first 90 days. It aims to ground new hires in the company culture, environment, and their role while providing them with the necessary tools for success and growth. In this phase, you invest in their personal and professional development, making sure they have the support they need to thrive.

The final phase, RETIRE, is a unique and forward-thinking aspect of the journey. It is about investing in the overall enrichment of employees, both inside and outside of the workplace. It acknowledges that a great culture extends beyond the time an employee spends with the company. It encourages organizations to consider how they want their departing employees to feel and what lasting impact they want to leave. In this phase, you consider what you want to gift your departing employees with—not just in terms of tangible benefits but also in terms of the lasting impact on their lives. How do you want them to feel about their time with your company, and what will they say about their experience?

Throughout this journey, the ultimate goal is to cultivate emotional commitment. By going beyond a transactional onboarding process, you show your employees that they are valued members of the organization. You create an inclusive and supportive environment that fosters growth, learning, and a sense of belonging. It's a journey that begins with the first hello and extends far beyond the final goodbye – a journey that leaves a positive and lasting impact on both the company and its people.

Establishing Emotional Commitment

Every employee at a company has a certain level of emotional commitment and that commitment increases or decreases depending on factors that may or may not seem relevant.

Emotional commitment is the level of personal dedication, passion, and attachment that an individual has towards a particular organization, brand, mission, product, or service. It's how someone feels connected, engaged, and invested in the entity, leading to a sense of loyalty and a willingness to go above and beyond in their involvement and contributions.

The ultimate goal with emotional commitment and where true success lies is before someone is hired and after leaving. You want them to shine such a positive light on their experience and time there that it attracts the next wave of humans that work together to achieve a mutually satisfying goal. When that happens, you create a legacy company where the true significance that someone brings is honored beyond their time there and lives on long after.

Emotional commitment ebbs and flows. The contributing factor to an employee deciding to quit comes down to:

- How many low points of emotional commitment vs. high points

- Timing of opportunities presented; for example, does an opportunity present itself during a low point or high point of emotional commitment.
- What is the contributing factor to each point of emotional commitment, regardless of its high or low; for example, did their closest colleague leave? Did a manager speak harshly to them, or did they feel appreciated after a project?
- Did the company do something ethical or unethical?

When emotional commitment begins and ends

Emotional commitment is a result of various micro factors that lead up to the macro experience.

From the moment someone applies for a job, emotional commitment begins to take shape. A level of emotion is already ignited as they envision themselves pursuing the opportunities and experiences that have been shared about your company.

As an employer, you have the opportunity to sow the seeds of emotional commitment in one or two crucial places: when someone applies for a job with your company, or when they connect with your brand, mission, product, or service. These initial touch points can play a significant role in establishing a strong emotional connection that can grow throughout the hiring process and beyond.

Emotional commitment is lower or nonexistent right before someone quits, which can be hard to predict; what typically happens is they are usually just doing what they need to do to get by because they are no longer emotionally committed to the job. They do the job for a factor that being employed provides for them, whether it is money, time, or security until something else comes along.

Great managers and leaders have been able to intuitively sense when someone is losing emotional commitment and is able to have an open conversation about what that people are experiencing.

The tie to emotional commitment

While this might not be the complete list, here are some core areas that emotional commitment yields and what could be missing if it starts to fade:

- **Energy:** the amount of energy one puts into something
- **Creativity:** the creative flow someone has to offer
- **Dialogue:** the amount of conversation one is willing to have
- **Ideas:** the amount of ideas someone is willing to share
- **Problem-solving:** the desire to find a solution to a particular problem or situation

- **Perspective:** offering a different perspective to a situation
- **Collaboration:** the willingness or ability to collaborate with others
- **Engagement:** the amount of involvement one has.
- **Attention / Being Present:** the desire to give prime attention to something.

How to Create Emotional Commitment

There are so many emotional touch points we experience in an hour, day, week, and month. Because of that, creating or establishing emotional commitment can be a bit tricky, however, consistency with the following makes a huge difference:

Use Humanity: All humans want to be treated like human. They want to be seen, heard and witnessed. They desire a level of kindness and grace to be given. This is key.

Show Appreciation: This is the start of emotional commitment. Going back to where emotional commitment starts at the job posting and often time the company brand. Somehow you've made that person feel appreciated enough to want to engage.

Build Trust: I've spoken about this in my Culture 101 Crash Course. There are two for sure ways to build trust as a leader and possibly a brand. (1) Do what you say you are going to do, consistently and (2) Show you care about others outside your direct sphere of influence. While it sounds simple enough, the duality our humanity offers some complications.

Show Emotion: It's how we connect on a deeper level as humans. When we express our emotions in a healthy way, we create space for others to do the same. This healthy exchange and interaction are key to building bonds and relationships. The downside is when emotion is expressed in a negative or manipulative way. Claiming that one is being their authentic self doesn't justify a lack of emotional awareness and maturity. If no one has said this, being authentic doesn't give permission to be an ass and treat others unkindly.

Cultivating emotional commitment is one of the most effective means to enhance a positive workplace environment and drive business success.

Start New Hires On Wednesdays

With over a decade of experience in People Ops and having onboarded over 500 employees, I've found that starting on Wednesdays gives people space and time to accept and acclimate to a new environment.

Most new hires are eager to prove their value and worth, often taking on too much and becoming overstimulated.

By starting on Wednesdays, it ensures a smoother onboarding experience where participants are engaged and have time to settle into their week. It also shortens the week, minimizing stress while providing a proper transition into onboarding and the work environment.

Considering that Mondays often receive a bad reputation in most workplaces and starting a new job is one of the top stressors in life, the culture-conscious choice to start new hires on Wednesdays is a win-win and truly changes the game.

Creating an exceptional welcome and onboarding experience doesn't necessarily require a large budget or abundant resources. I've personally developed some of the best onboarding programs with limited to no budget or resources.

The key lies in the intention behind it and the humanity you bring to the process. When you approach onboarding with genuine concern for the well-being and development of your new hires, the rewards will extend far beyond measurable outcomes.

Begin Here

Recap:

- Welcoming is a universal practice that impacts workplace culture significantly, as it sets the tone for a new hire's overall experience and their longevity in the organization.
- The impact of welcoming begins even before a new hire's actual arrival, with the energy and thoughtfulness put into their onboarding experience being palpable.
- The "Hello-to-Hire, Inspire, & Retire" journey emphasizes a strategic and holistic approach to welcoming new hires, divided into three phases: HELLO-to-HIRE, INSPIRE, and RETIRE.
- Emotional commitment is influenced by various micro factors that contribute to an employee's overall experience in the workplace.
- Creating emotional commitment yields positive elements such as energy, creativity, dialogue, ideas, problem-solving, perspective, collaboration, engagement, and attention.
- The culture-conscious choice of starting on Wednesdays can lead to a smoother onboarding experience and positively impact a new hire's emotional commitment to the organization.

Reflection Question:

How can you integrate the "Hello-to-Hire, Inspire, & Retire" journey into your organization's onboarding process to enhance emotional commitment and employee retention?

Action

Develop or revise your comprehensive onboarding plan that extends beyond the first 90 days to foster emotional commitment and support personal and professional growth.

You lead how you live.

CHAPTER 6

LEAD LIKE YOU GIVE A SHIT

Day three came. It was time to share my pregnancy news with my manager.

We met first thing in the morning, as we usually did during her non-travel days. We went over the day's tasks; she'd ask if I needed anything and I did the same. Our 30-minute morning check-ins helped establish my main tasks for the day.

As I reflect on that moment, I remember the warmth of her office and the genuine smile on her face. She was always so present with me.

I didn't cry, although I felt my face flushing over. I found myself looking down slightly, as if I had done something wrong, when I shared my news with her.

What happened next changed my life forever and completely shifted how I viewed leadership.

As I looked up to see what her response would be, it was almost as if she had known. A big smile took over and grew even bigger. She congratulated me wholeheartedly and said it was amazing news and assured me that the team would support me in any way they could. In that moment, my energy shifted, and I couldn't help but smile back at her, making solid eye contact. I had made a vow during my job interview to always give my best, and reinstated it again in that moment.

I later shared this interaction with the recruiter who brought me in, who was equally excited and supportive.

This kind and supportive leadership continued throughout my time there, setting the bar so high for other leaders that some might have tapped out.

At that point, my manager, nor anyone on the team, had any idea that I was homeless. Shortly after I started, I had to take time off to appear in a court room in Oakland, CA as Jane Doe to testify against a man who had sexually assaulted me when I was 15. Despite not being able to afford to take the day off, I felt safe, cared for, and seen by my manager and team.

The challenges continued, including a difficult custody battle where I had to share parts of my story with Valerie and explain how I would make up for the time off.

Valerie transformed from being just a manager to becoming my life mentor. She was more than a Director of Oncology; she genuinely cared about me and invested in my well-being above and beyond her role.

Valerie changed not only my life but also the lives of my children.

Her compassionate and supportive leadership left a lasting impact that I will forever cherish.

There are over 15,000 books offering advice on becoming a great leader. I don't aim to repeat what has been written, but in parallel with my experience and interactions I want to share something that might be an introduction to the idea or a reminder of true leadership.

My business mantra is also my leadership mantra: "we are roots to the tree of which we will never experience shade." This means we invest, spend time with, help lay the foundation, empower, give, and engage all with a deep knowingness that we might not fully see how what we are doing will manifest in the future. We know goodness will come from it and we are okay with not being witness to or enjoying the harvest. This allows us to go in unattached but fully engaged in helping our client partners solve some of their toughest problems with all routes leading to the culture. This is how we chose to show up as leaders every day.

It's important to distinguish a leader from a leader with a title. The two live drastically different lives. I'm sure you can think of a few people in each category and you might even see yourself in one as well.

As a leader, you hold a great responsibility and gift. I want to share ways in which you can lead with empowerment that will have a direct and positive affect on your company culture and beyond.

Similar to my story, Valerie's leadership was well underway before I showed up, yet it was exactly what I needed and it continues to be a gift that I pass on in my own version of leadership style.

The Hybrid Leader

In the realm of leadership, there exists a dichotomy that I address in my skill-building workshop called LIT (Leaders in Training).

The first thing I emphasize is the distinction between leadership and management. While both are important, they are different roles with distinct expectations and outcomes. However, in today's fast-paced workplace, some individuals find themselves having to juggle both responsibilities.

I don't object to people taking on both leadership and management roles, but the challenge arises when they fail to recognize the differences and aren't adequately equipped to excel in either position.

You are either a leader with management responsibilities or a manager with leadership expectations.

If someone can effectively perform both roles, that's excellent. However, the trap of being a hybrid leader can lead to shortcomings. This model can erode confidence in one's ability to grow in either area and create a lack of trust within the organization if one of the roles receives insufficient attention.

No matter which one you are one core element is needed: trust.

There are two sure ways to build trust:

1. Consistently do what you say you will do.
2. Show that you genuinely care and have concern for others beyond your immediate sphere of influence.

Let's go deeper into both.

Do what you say you are going to do consistently.

Throughout history, societies have relied heavily on recognizing patterns in weather, animal behaviors, and other factors for their survival. For instance, identifying a pattern of drought would prompt them to start saving and preparing for the upcoming season.

In a similar vein, your company culture tracks leadership patterns and makes decisions based on observed behaviors, even with limited visibility into the variables at play. Imagine taking a road trip, and the driver starts driving erratically, missing key turns, and ignoring mile markers. In a matter of moments, you might question if they know where they are going, if they know what they are doing, and if you are safe. All of these questions are based on the pattern you are witnessing.

Consistency is a rhythmic pattern that provides the culture with predictability.

As a leader, consistency plays a pivotal role in shaping the culture of your organization. Where you begin your journey to consistency doesn't matter as much as staying committed to it. Whether it's the set times for starting and ending your workday or how you greet everyone, right down to your choice of tea or coffee, these consistent actions send powerful signals to the culture.

Consistency enables the culture to track the pattern, providing predictability, and predictability, in turn, increases the chances of survival and success. Just like recognizing patterns helped societies thrive in the past, your consistent leadership fosters an environment of trust and stability, laying a solid foundation for your team's growth and overall prosperity.

Doing what you say you are going to do gives the culture predictability and increases trust. The opposite erodes trust.

If you are a new leader or want to gain trust, I recommend understanding your internal reality of your behaviors and patterns. If you struggle with timeliness, be mindful of committing to solid deadlines for projects. Instead, give a range in which you can have something done, openly discuss your focus on timeliness as a leader, and if you don't meet the discussed timeframe, acknowledge it and do your best to correct it quickly.

The best thing about the culture is that it loves consistency and doesn't demand perfection. So, if you find that you struggle in this area, remember to be kind to yourself. Tap into your self-awareness and start the inward work that will yield abundant outward results.

The culture is just as forgiving as you are to yourself.

Read that again.

The culture is just as forgiving as you are to yourself.

Embracing forgiveness and grace on this journey, starting with self, can be a powerful way to nurture a positive and thriving culture that supports everyone's growth and development.

Show that you care about others beyond those in your sphere of influence.

This one is simple and complex as it has to do with how you view others by how you view yourself.

If you reflect on some of the leaders you most admire, you'll notice a shared quality among them: an undeniable care for others—and not just for a specific group, but for all people.

When you show genuine concern for those who can offer you nothing in return or who have no direct relevance to your current situation, it highlights compassion.

What you say and do significantly shapes the organizational culture. The culture pays close attention to how you speak about others. Do you communicate from a space of compassion or judgment?

The culture can quickly identify both, and whichever one is most consistent, the culture will respond to.

I find this to be challenging for most leaders to do, and it perfectly sets the stage for exploring the next core aspect of leadership.

Leaders cannot give what they don't have.

Leadership often hinges on a simple yet often overlooked concept, and it's one of the biggest reasons why leaders fail.

While some might believe that leaders fail due to a lack of fundamental leadership skills, the truth is that significance doesn't come from a toolbox full of items, but from a few essential ones.

The bottom line is this: you can't give what you don't have. Whatever you cultivate within yourself as a human being will inevitably manifest in your leadership.

A beautiful story shared by Wayne Dyer perfectly illustrates this point. He asked an audience, "If I were to squeeze an orange, what would come out?" The audience chuckled, thinking it was a trick question. After a moment of silence, Dr. Dyer provided the answer: "Orange juice."

He then posed more seemingly tricky questions: "Does apple juice come out when I squeeze an orange? Mango juice? Pineapple juice?" The audience laughed and replied with a resounding, "No."

Finally, Dr. Dyer asked the seemingly elementary question: "Why, then, when I squeeze this orange, does orange juice come out?"

Silence filled the room before Dr. Dyer answered with profound simplicity: "Because that's what's inside."

As a leader, you face a myriad of pressures, expectations, challenges, and opportunities both in the workplace and in your personal life. The way you respond to these situations is a reflection of what resides within you.

If anger, frustration, or rudeness come out in your actions and interactions, it's because those emotions exist within you. On the other hand, if kindness, compassion, understanding, and patience emanate from you, it's because they are part of your inner makeup.

The human experience is not compartmentalized between the title of "leader" and other roles in your life. Taking care of the whole human is key to effective leadership.

When leaders show up differently in their workplace and home life, they experience energy whiplash. It's akin to the scene from the movie "Mrs. Doubtfire," where the main character, Daniel Hillard, portrayed by Robin Williams, assumes the persona of a British nanny to spend time with his kids. In a hilarious but poignant moment, he finds himself juggling both roles at the same restaurant, switching from one persona to another, until his true identity is exposed.

This movie scene serves as an excellent analogy for leaders who aren't consistent in every aspect of their lives. When you continuously switch between different personas, it becomes challenging to maintain authenticity and trust with your team and others around you.

If there's one crucial takeaway from this book, let it be this: you cannot give what you don't have. It is imperative to prioritize evolved self-care, nurture yourself with kind words, and dispel negative thoughts that only breed doubt and judgment, consuming valuable mental space.

As leaders, what you give to the world reflects the vibrational aspects of our humanity. If you feed the world with lower vibrational emotions, we'll find those same energies manifesting in your surroundings.

Behind closed doors, I've held space for CEOs and leaders who constantly put pressure on themselves to maintain an image and live up to a title lives closely with the ego. In those private moments, they break down, seeking guidance while grappling with their true selves, often navigating alone.

Self-care is not a luxury; it is a necessity. By taking care of ourselves, we not only benefit personally but also create a positive ripple effect on others. It exemplifies the essence of Ubuntu, a concept I'll delve into further later on.

So, please, practice self-care. You owe it to yourself, and others around you will benefit greatly from you becoming the best version of you. In the true spirit of Ubuntu, the better you are, the better we all become.

Self Care

The best leaders do it best.

They understand that pushing themselves beyond their limits leads to ineffectiveness, poor decision-making, and negative relationships.

They know that not taking care of oneself isn't a badge of honor or a rite of passage. Instead, it can lead to devastating health news, broken relationships, a negative self-image, and feelings of hopelessness.

This may sound dark and deep, but it's a reality many face. When leaders feel the weight of carrying everything without caring for themselves, they push themselves past human limits.

Just like the airlines' safety instructions, put your own masks on first before assisting others. Self-care goes beyond occasional massages or vacations; it is a continuous and intentional ritual that revolves around nurturing oneself.

Self-care wasn't taught or modeled for many of us growing up. Society emphasized hard work, associating worth with productivity, and rewarding performance over personal growth. In a world that values conformity, convenience, and comfort, overworking and taking work on vacations seemed normal.

We even downplay the importance of self-care when discussing death, saying, "rest in peace" as if peace is only attainable in death. However, it is in our daily lives that we need peace the most, making self-care essential.

My self-care workshop defines self-care simply as "the care of oneself." To delve deeper, we explore four main and expansive areas of self-care:

Emotionally:

Being aware of and caring for one's emotions and feelings.

This might look like checking in with one's emotions and understanding the reasons behind them. Asking questions to gain insight into strong emotions helps with reflection and healing. Redirecting emotional energy towards positive outcomes proves beneficial. When feeling stuck, writing down thoughts and feelings can provide perspective and clarity.

Physically:

Taking care of the body's physical needs, such as movement, hydration, and nourishment.

Listening to the body and studying its needs are crucial components of self-care. Developing a love for one's body and spending time outdoors barefoot, connecting with nature's energy, which fosters grounding and vitality. Staying hydrated and engaging in physical activities that nourish the body are vital. Being mindful of food intake and responding to the body's signals ensures overall well-being.

Mentally:

Engaging in positive self-talk, clearing unhelpful thoughts, and being mindful of the information consumed.

This might look like practicing positive self-talk. Acknowledging and clearing thoughts that hinder personal growth and well-being is necessary. Avoiding absolute statements about oneself and instead encouraging open dialogue fosters a healthy mental state. Being mindful of the information and media consumed can impact mental well-being positively.

Spiritually:

Recognizing and nurturing one's spiritual essence, connecting with higher powers or spiritual energies, and exploring spiritual beliefs and practices.

Recognizing one's spiritual essence and embracing the human experience is a vital aspect of self-care. Connecting with higher powers, whether it's God, the Universe, or other spiritual energies, can provide a sense of purpose and peace. Regular meditation and surrounding oneself with meaningful objects aid in spiritual connection. Engaging in deep conversations about spirituality and learning about different cultural practices enriches spiritual understanding.

As a mother of six, entrepreneur of a few businesses and actively participating in my community, I prioritize self-care through solo retreats. I carve out three to five days to find space and peace, an essential need due to my many roles and responsibilities.

Remember, there is no one-size-fits-all approach to self-care. Each person's journey is unique, and what works for someone else may not work for you. Embrace your way, be adaptable as life evolves, and explore what practices resonate with your well-being. As a leader, embarking on this journey of self-care is immensely impactful and essential for navigating the complexities of life and leadership successfully.

What Your Culture Needs from Leaders

When it comes to effective leadership, understanding the expectations of your culture is crucial. Fortunately, these expectations are remarkably consistent across different contexts.

Here are the key elements your culture seeks from its leaders.

People Investment

Your culture seeks more than just perks and paychecks; they want to feel truly invested in. They desire to be recognized as individuals empowered to set and achieve their goals. Considering that most of their time is spent in the workplace, having leaders who can inspire greatness from within becomes a crucial investment in the future of your company.

Safety

Feeling safe in the workplace is of utmost importance to your culture, and the employees look to leadership to ensure this. Transparent communication fosters a sense of security, building trust and strong connections. Any inconsistencies in providing a safe environment can be challenging to recover from.

Direction

Leaders are expected to provide clear direction to the culture, allowing them to work with purpose and avoid feeling lost or unproductive.

Nothing leaves the culture feeling more adrift than a lack of direction, spinning in circles with nothing tangible to show for our efforts. Leaders play a crucial role in providing clarity and purpose to the culture, helping them navigate their roles with confidence.

Empathy

The culture seeks leadership that genuinely cares about the culture's well-being and understands their experiences. Empathy becomes the thread that connects leaders with their teams, providing valuable insights to handle any challenges that may arise.

Humanity

Leaders are human too, and showcasing that humanity is a valuable trait. Vulnerability, humility, and compassion are qualities highly appreciated by your people. Such characteristics create an environment where employees feel supported and at ease.

Your culture's expectations are clear and fundamental to building a strong, positive, and productive work environment. Meeting these expectations is essential for leaders aiming to cultivate trust and growth within their organizations.

Remember as a leader, the ego reacts, humanity responds.

What Leaders Need

Good leaders become great leaders because of their desire to serve others and lead them to greatness.

Leaders become toxic leaders because of their ego, desire for self-preservation and willingness to be served.

Know how to recognize the two.

Each leader you bring on needs the following:

Coaching

Steph Curry, Serena Williams, Jimmy Garoppolo, Michael Jordan, Joe Montana, Lionel Messi, Larry Bird, and Mohamad Ali are all iconic and greatly talented athletes. However, what you rarely saw in their journey to success was the instrumental role played by their coaches—the guiding figures in the background who offered support, encouragement, a listening ear, and sometimes even a shoulder to cry on.

In the same way, when you set up a leader within your company, it's essential to partner them with a coach from outside the organization. This approach ensures that leaders continuously develop both personally and professionally, fostering growth inside and outside of the workplace.

Every leader in your company, including yourself, can greatly benefit from having a coach, especially during the early stages of their leadership journey. A coach helps them reflect on their experiences, focus on their development as leaders, and make valuable progress.

Teaming your leadership layer with coaches is a powerful retention strategy that demonstrates your investment in their growth and success. By finding a coach and making it clear that they will support your leaders in any way they need, you provide an opportunity for exceptional outcomes and continued development.

When interviewing and bringing on new leaders, emphasize the importance of healthy leadership and express your commitment to investing in their growth. Offer them the support of a monthly coach for their first year, setting the stage for their leadership journey in the organization.

By recognizing the value of coaching and investing in your leaders' development, you pave the way for their success and contribute to a thriving and dynamic work culture. Just as great athletes rely on their coaches to achieve excellence, your leaders can soar to new heights with the support of a dedicated coach by their side.

Mentoring

Mentors are different than coaches. Mentors are individuals who have hands-on experience in the same or similar roles as your leaders. A mentor should possess a deeper understanding of the specific area and have more extensive expertise in that domain. Their role is to provide invaluable insights, serve as a sounding board for ideas, and offer constructive feedback based on their own journey.

Unlike coaching, which may require a formal arrangement and external sourcing, mentorship relationships are often built on mutual interest and a genuine desire to learn and grow. Leaders can seek out mentors on their own, allowing the relationship to develop organically and authentically.

My mentor is almost 80 years young and has seen me through my journey of homelessness. At a glance, you might see us as an unlikely pair, yet she has been instrumental in my professional and personal success.

She has helped me vision deeper when I felt there was no light to see where I was going. Her wisdom balanced beautifully with the hands-on guidance from my coach, who helped me anchor and extract the greatness within.

Encouraging leaders to proactively seek out mentors and engage in regular meetings fosters a supportive environment for continuous learning and development. Mentoring offers a unique perspective that complements the coaching process, making it an indispensable component of a comprehensive leadership development program.

Feedback

Having a C-level, Executive or Director title doesn't exempt anyone from needing feedback. Unfortunately, giving and receiving feedback is something many people shy away from or struggle with, leading them to avoid addressing issues until they escalate to a critical point.

Your leaders crave both affirming and constructive feedback to guide their actions and validate their efforts. If you find yourself struggling to provide effective feedback, don't hesitate to take action. Consider taking a class, hiring a coach, or even practicing in front of a mirror to enhance your feedback skills. Remember, giving valuable feedback is crucial—don't overlook this responsibility, as your leaders truly need it to thrive and grow.

Appreciation

It is essential for your leaders to feel appreciated for the work they do. Just as you expect your leaders to ensure their team members feel valued and recognized, you must do the same for them.

I've written a whole chapter on Appreciation that will provide some great ways to show appreciation. However, the key point is that you must genuinely appreciate and acknowledge your leaders' efforts to foster a positive and motivated work environment.

Your leaders can't give what they don't have. They can't effectively support others if they neglect their own well-being. Emphasize and practice the importance of self-care within your organization. This not only fosters balance in their work-life but also in their personal lives outside of the workplace. Telling them to practice self-care might not be enough, as many won't prioritize it due to feelings of guilt and an overwhelming to-do list.

As a leader, your responsibility is to convince your leaders that taking care of themselves is crucial. Regardless of the guilt or tasks, they must make time for self-care. Encourage them to find healthy ways to decompress and nurture themselves. Remember, your actions speak louder than words, so lead by example and show your leaders that self-care is a vital aspect of a successful and sustainable leadership journey.

Diverse Leadership

Diversity is the state of being different or varied, encompassing a range of unique elements, individuals, or groups that contribute to the richness and variety of a particular context, community, or society.

This means you want leadership with diverse stories and experiences woven throughout their journey. Embrace the tapestry of humanity by connecting and unifying diverse leaders. Look for individuals who are non-traditional thinkers or have unique perspectives. When you strike the right balance with diverse leadership, alignment happens, and the results are dynamic.

Embracing diversity within your leadership team leads to a thriving and innovative environment where everyone can contribute their best. Welcome true diversity and watch your leaders and organization flourish.

Begin Here

One of my favorite exercises to give leaders is a fusion of tactical and intuitive thinking. I ask them to think of a leader they greatly admire and look up to, whether dead, alive, fictional, or non-fictional—it doesn't matter.

I tell ask them to consider that leadership style and use it as a grounding for their own as they level up as a leader.

This tiny yet impactful exercise is powerful because it allows you to immerse yourself in the space of the leader you most connect with and think about how they would handle or approach a situation.

Recap:

- There is a difference between a leader and a leader with a title.
- The "Hybrid Leader" is someone who combines both leadership and management responsibilities.
- Building trust through consistency and genuine care for others who aren't in direct proximity to you is crucial for effective leadership.
- Leaders cannot give what they don't have and must prioritize self-care to foster a positive work environment.
- The culture needs leaders that invest in their people, create safety, give clear direction, practice empathy, and honor humanity.

- Leaders need coaching, mentoring, constructive feedback, appreciation, and to be surrounded by diverse leadership to thrive and succeed.

Reflective Question

Who is a leader you admire? Which aspects of their leadership can you incorporate to enhance your own leadership approach?

Action

Partner your company's leaders with external coaches to support their continuous growth and development.

The Observer

I am the observer observing the observation.
Ego doesn't exist here.
From this view, I am able to see all,
Hate, love, anger, joy, and fear.

I can see what is happening, and I watch it take place.
I can see what we are doing to our humanity, our planet, the human race.
When the human gets mad, something boils inside; there isn't a healing that takes place; it's often hate and pride.

Everything has its life cycle, and things we must let go.
For some, it happens fast; for others, it's slow.
When we don't let go,
Something infectious—it grows deep within from inside.
Some come out to play—some run and hide.

I am the observer observing the observation.
Come quick, take a look; most of what we believe is gifted, and there's always a hook.
If harboring anger worked, our problems would be solved.
Yet it does the opposite, and hope and change it dissolves.
We think we are making a difference—we convinced ourselves so,
Yet, with a heavily medicated, over-anxious being, we continue to sow,
Sowing seeds that are poisonous and have little nutrition and taste.
Seeds that won't yield change for the whole human race.

Ego has got us, but we won't admit it—we fear that true change won't be worth it.
That it will be anticlimactic.
So, we wade in the waters all covered in shit; we wade in the waters and invite others in it.
Tupac once said, "change the way we eat, change the way we live, change the way we treat each other.
We're too busy staying the same to have any change to give.

I am the observer observing the observation; I have nothing to gain.
As I watch the momentum go on, this runaway train.

I see the light come in, and ego quickly shuts it out.
I see the light come in, and you quickly suck it out.
You say you want equality and things to be fair.
Equality is relative and is subjective to the one who is there.
Life isn't designed with fairness in mind;
It's all about balance—even time is divine.
What we've been facing is ancient; it's been here a while.
It's the same type of outfit, just a different style.

I am the observer observing the observation.
I can offer you hope.
Yet, ego reacts angrily, and it's always a nope.
I try and teach you something new, but you don't get it, you don't see.

You're wrapped up in what you believe and discredit your knowing.
You are having a human experience—its easy to forget.
This human experience is hard and can create some conflict,
But I tell you this—everything you've asked has been given.
Everything you need is here to really start livin'.

You thought it was in material things, and you don't have it half wrong,
But it's in the non-material where things are created,
Where you get chills from a song.
I want to help guide your mind; I really do.
But as the observer observing the observation,
This is something only you can do.

CHAPTER 7

APPRECIATE LIKE YOU GIVE A SHIT

I was seven months pregnant when my team surprised me with a baby shower. At that time, I had moved out of the shelter and was living in transitional housing. Although the apartment was furnished with the basics, I still needed items for my baby.

Walking into the conference room, I was greeted by cheerful yellow and green balloons, a beautifully decorated cake, and a table with gifts and cards. I had attended other baby showers for some employees as there was a baby boom at our company; most of the babies were due within a month of each other.

The gifts I received were incredibly valuable as they covered much-needed essentials and I didn't need to get them used out of the donation bins.

As we celebrated, I found myself speaking into existence the nursery as if I had a place to call my own. The joy of the moment and the warmth of my team made me hopeful, even during this transitional period in my life.

My team members became my biggest supporters without fully knowing the intricacies of my personal situation.

To this day, they might never fully grasp just how much their support meant to me. Their thoughtful actions made me feel deeply appreciated.

Underappreciated Appreciation

Appreciation, a simple yet essential concept, often goes unnoticed in the workplace. Companies often prioritize employee engagement, aiming to swiftly connect it to return on investment and the overall employee experience.

When organizations bring me in, they usually have specific requests or desires from the culture. They want to see changes in behavior, the adoption of company values, or increased engagement and productivity in their work.

However, the truth is that the most significant reason people resist these changes is that they don't feel appreciated.

Despite all the efforts to drive engagement and productivity, the missing ingredient is often genuine appreciation. Employees yearn to be valued and recognized for their contributions and efforts. When they don't receive the appreciation they deserve, it affects their willingness to embrace positive changes and align with the company's vision. This is one of the areas that impacts emotional commitment.

Imagine a workplace where employees feel genuinely appreciated for their hard work, energy, and contribution. In such an environment, motivation soars and employees become more committed and enthusiastic about their roles. The ripple effect of appreciation extends far beyond the individual; it positively impacts team dynamics and overall company culture.

Leaders must recognize that appreciation is not just a feel-good gesture; it is a powerful driver of employee engagement and performance. When employees feel valued and appreciated, they are more likely to use the energy they bring to the workplace efficiently.

By prioritizing appreciation, we create a workplace where positive change is embraced, and individuals are motivated to go above and beyond, ultimately leading to a thriving and successful organization.

Your People Need Water

A missionary arrived in a rural African tribe to teach the people about God. Standing in the middle of the village, he opened his bible and started to preach. At one point in his message he kept saying, "God loves you! Jesus loves you! He loves you so much!"

A tribesman stood up and replied, "Don't tell us about a God who loves us when we have no water."

At that very moment the missionary closed his bible and started digging wells in this rural tribe in Africa.

Many employees lack the essential and simple needs to thrive, yet companies expect them to perform, trust, and act in ways that require a solid foundation.

Showing appreciation to your people doesn't demand extravagant gestures. It only takes a small effort to make someone feel valued and appreciated. However, it requires a genuine recognition of their humanity and consistent efforts to demonstrate that appreciation.

There have been many times where companies have brought me in to address a specific behavior pattern within their company culture; the lack of being appreciated consistently comes up.

The culture feels the demand of having to produce and yield high-end results, but when it comes to feeling appreciated, the leaders and the company miss the mark.

Next to leadership self-care, appreciation is top on the list of a for sure way to keep your company culture from going to shit.

In this next part, I am going to break down how appreciation within the workplace is a game changer as well as provide you with some great resources to get started.

Breaking down Appreciation:

Employee engagement surveys have become a popular trend over the past few decades. These surveys are designed to assess and measure the level of engagement, satisfaction, and overall well-being of employees within an organization. The primary goal of conducting engagement surveys is to gather feedback from employees, understand their perspectives, and identify areas of improvement to enhance the work environment and overall employee experience.

However, amidst the trend and focus on engagement, many companies have overlooked a crucial factor that precedes engagement: appreciation.

The cycle of how appreciation and engagement are linked goes as follows: companies desire engaged employees, and employees, in turn, want to feel appreciated. To achieve both, it's essential to follow these steps:

(1) Appreciation —> (2) Feedback —> (3) Emotional Commitment —> (4) Engagement

1. Feeling appreciated is a game-changer. It means acknowledging and honoring employees for their work, energy, effort, and unique qualities. When employees feel genuinely appreciated in ways that resonate with them, they become more receptive to directions and feel empowered to contribute their ideas.

2. Once people feel appreciated, giving and receiving feedback becomes easier. Not many enjoy receiving solely negative feedback. Lack of appreciation can make constructive feedback challenging to give and receive. Balancing constructive feedback with acknowledgment of their accomplishments fosters a more positive feedback culture.

3. Emotional commitment significantly depends on the feedback culture in the organization. A supportive feedback loop can foster strong emotional commitment among employees.

4. Emotional commitment is directly tied to engagement. When someone is newly hired, their emotional commitment to the organization is usually high. If an employee becomes disengaged or considers leaving, their emotional commitment declines.

By understanding and implementing this cycle of appreciation, feedback, emotional commitment, and engagement, companies can create a thriving work environment where employees feel valued, motivated, and committed to contributing their best efforts. Prioritizing appreciation lays the foundation for building a more engaged and fulfilled workforce.

Appreciation Outweighs Engagement

Engagement is the product of appreciation. It serves as the foundation for productivity, innovation, creativity, and groundbreaking ideas.

When you genuinely appreciate someone, you communicate that you recognize and value their inherent complexity. Though it may sound abstract, it simply means acknowledging their humanity and treating them with kindness, even when you have nothing else to offer in that moment.

Companies might find it easier to focus solely on employee engagement, assuming it to be the key factor. However, the truth is that it costs more to prioritize engagement solely over ensuring that employees feel appreciated.

In a study that revealed that 79% of employees leave their jobs because they don't feel appreciated. Employee appreciation is a crucial aspect that isn't typically taught in business school, yet it holds power over tremendous outcomes.

Listen, you've invested considerable effort into building your remarkable company, focusing on the other critical areas that shape your culture; don't let the opportunity to show appreciation slip away. Appreciation doesn't have to cost anything monetarily; it can be as simple as heartfelt acknowledgment. However, it will yield profound results that will enhance your business's success.

If you're wondering why more companies aren't prioritizing appreciation, it's because they either lack knowledge or mistakenly believe that solely focusing on the product, service, and profitability will lead to the desired outcomes. However, this mindset often produces the opposite effect.

It all comes down to the people. It always has and always will. I cannot emphasize this enough: prioritize your people and demonstrate that they are genuinely appreciated.

Let me quickly define what prioritizing your people means from a cultural perspective. It means considering the impact on people in every decision being made and keeping their well-being in parallel with the "what" and "how" of workplace happenings.

Prioritizing your people doesn't mean granting every request they make, as they might need more business context and understanding behind certain decisions. It's about finding a balance between meeting their needs and aligning them with the organization's overall objectives.

In all the assessments we've conducted, a direct correlation between engagement and appreciation has been observed. Your employees want to feel appreciated first before they can fully engage.

The Truth About Appreciation

When my husband and I were going through our pre-marital counseling, our guide introduced us to a book that would profoundly impact our relationship: *The Five Love Languages* by Dr. Gary Chapman. I immersed myself in this book, reading it cover to cover. It was amazing.

Dr. Chapman proposes that in order for a healthy relationship to succeed, each person must feel loved by the other, and the best way to do that is to speak each other's "love language" often and frequently. Dr. Chapman's research suggests that the same "love languages" that help build successful relationships can be transferred into the workplace to ensure healthy workplace relationships. Instead of calling them "love languages," he dubbed them "appreciation languages," and they are just as effective. In the final part of this chapter, I'd like to share with you these languages and what they mean.

Five Ways to Appreciate

There are five key ways that employees like to be appreciated. Most people have a dominant appreciation preference; some have two. Nevertheless, it's essential to know what they are and what they mean, and how to utilize them within the workplace.

I've summerized some key learnings from The 5 Langugages of Appreciation in the Wrkplace by Gary Chapman & Paul White.

Words

Employees that like to receive appreciation through written and verbal expressions and need to be affirmed with positive, encouraging words - the opposite is true as well. If you bombard them with negative words or harsh criticism, they will take it to heart and become demotivated. Conversely, using harsh or negative language can deeply impact someone who values this form of appreciation.

How to do It

Effective verbal praise hinges on being specific and meaningful. For instance, instead of a general "good job, everyone," you might say, "I truly appreciate how you structured the project; it showcases your meticulous attention to detail."

Affirmation of Character moves beyond performance, delving into a person's core nature. For example, you could tell Marlee, "Your kindness and consideration shine through when you interact with our customers."

Praising Personality involves highlighting positive traits, like optimism, organization, and planning abilities. For instance, you might express, "Your vibrant and upbeat energy as I enter the office sets the perfect tone for my day."

When to do It

- **Individual Settings:** Offering praise one-on-one holds immense value. It's direct, effective, and immediately reinforces positive behavior.
- **Public Praise:** Recognizing someone's achievements in front of others signifies your appreciation. It communicates, "I value your contributions." Opt for smaller groups for a more personal touch.
- **Written:** A heartfelt email or chat acknowledging a co-worker's effort, like a "great job" or "that presentation was fire," can make their day. When appropriate, use emojis.
- **Public Acknowledgment:** While public praise can be impactful, be mindful of the person's comfort level with such attention. It's especially fitting for significant accomplishments or events.

Time

These individuals value appreciation through quality time enjoy spending meaningful moments with others. For them, feeling appreciated involves receiving undivided attention and genuine connection. Whether it's collaborating on a project or simply engaging in a conversation, these moments hold significant value.

On the other hand, if you are preoccupied with texting or emailing while spending time with someone who cherishes quality time, it can lead to feelings of being ignored or unimportant, triggering negative emotions. Being fully present and attentive is crucial for demonstrating appreciation to individuals who resonate with this language.

How to do it

- **Meaningful Conversations**: Engage in quality conversations, free of distractions. Make eye contact, conversational body language, and practice active listening.
- **Small Group Discussions**: Arrange a small group dialogue. This setting is ideal for those who value a communal exchange of ideas. It could be a team discussion or a group outing.
- **Collaborative Project Work**: Working closely together on a project can foster a strong bond. The collaborative effort strengthens the relationship and enhances the work outcome.

- **Breaking Bread Together**: Sharing a meal over lunch, tea, or coffee offers a relaxed atmosphere for meaningful conversations.

How to do it

- **Use Nature**: Nature walks can provide an excellent backdrop for heart-to-heart conversations. If they value one-on-one time, arrange a walk and talk. If they value group dynamics, invite a few companions.
- **Event Planning**: Organize an off-site retreat or a team-building event. Such occasions build rapport and offer a change of pace and environment. Be mindful of centering events around alcohol, as that can be exclusive and lead to possible challenges later.
- **Unwind with Fun**:. Engaging in enjoyable activities outside the office can lead to deeper connections.

Gifts

Some individuals feel appreciated by giving and receiving thoughtful gifts. In a workplace context, this might entail offering a dinner card as a gesture of appreciation or providing tickets to a sporting event to acknowledge a job well done. For these individuals, useful and meaningful gifts hold significance and serve as a powerful way to show recognition.

This appreciation language is particularly enjoyable for me because once I understand someone's interests and preferences, I can select or create a gift that they will genuinely cherish and enjoy. It adds a personal touch to the act of appreciation, making it even more meaningful for both the giver and the recipient.

How to do it

- **Add Significance:** Attach the gift to a specific achievement or effort they made.
- **Value in Currency:** While money is a solid choice, opt for uniqueness if possible (like a gift card to their favorite store or a platform like GiftRocket).
- **Personal Touch:** Consider handpicked or homemade items; prioritize their preferences. Wrapping adds to the gesture.

When to do it

- When you genuinely want to express gratitude for their performance or a particular contribution.
- Keep it discreet unless the employee appreciates public acknowledgment.
- Consider sending gifts to their home rather than the workplace. A heartfelt handwritten note goes a long way, and receiving happy mail makes people happy.

- Offer the gift of time, such as leaving work early or providing paid time off upon project completion. Remember, a gift should be meaningful and enjoyable for the employee.

Being of Service

This appreciation language relates to individuals who feel most appreciated when action is taken to help them with a task or project. These people are doers. They believe that actions speak louder than words, and they demonstrate their appreciation by taking tangible steps to help and support others. Whether it's completing tasks or going the extra mile to assist a colleague, acts of service are their way of expressing and accepting appreciation.

Conversely, failing to follow through on commitments or promises can be deeply offensive to people who receive appreciation through acts of service. Reliability and consistency in actions are crucial to maintaining a positive relationship with them.

In the workplace, individuals with this appreciation language can be easily disheartened if their acts of service are overlooked or taken for granted. Recognizing their efforts and acknowledging the significance of their contributions can go a long way in nurturing their sense of appreciation and commitment.

How to do it

- **Ensure your capacity**: Prioritize your well-being before assisting others, much like putting on your mask first.
- **Seek permission:** Always, without exception, ask for permission before offering help. Refrain from assuming that assistance is needed or wanted.
- **Match their approach:** Carry out the task in the manner they prefer.
- **Commitment counts:** If you initiate a task, follow through on your commitment. Only make promises you intend to fulfill.

When to do it

- **Time-sensitive tasks**: Step in when you notice someone tackling a time-bound task, offering your assistance, or suggesting ways you could help.
- **Personal matters:** Extend your support outside of work, especially during life-changing events like childbirth or significant family transitions.
- **Pursue ambitions:** If feasible, assist them in achieving a personal or professional goal they've shared.

Touch

Individuals who relate to this appreciation language feel appreciated with a solid handshake, fist bump, high five, or even a hug. They also enjoy being in proximity of others.

When to do it

- **Intentional Handshake:** Offer a firm handshake while maintaining kind eye contact and a genuine smile.
- **Embrace:** Different kinds of hugs like the Bear Hug, Side Hug, High Fives, and Fist Bumps are wonderful, especially during celebrations or after completing a daunting task.
- **Pet Companionship**: Incorporating animals in the workplace can be a brilliant way to cater to this language, providing sensory touch experiences.
- **Sensory toys:** having sensory toys can be another effective way to cater to this language. I used to put different nick-nacks in the conference rooms and around the office - folks that vibed with this would always gravitate to them.

Where to do it

- **The Welcome:** Solid handshakes and firm hugs are perfect for greetings, farewells, or during emotionally charged moments.

Be sure your hugs are intentional, and feel free to find your preferred hug style for added comfort.

- **Non-Physical Interaction:** Your body language also plays a pivotal role. Stand squarely and maintain a reasonable distance from the other person to enhance the effect of your communication.

IMPORTANT: *If you are not comfortable with this language, it's okay to let the person know. In the workplace, we want to make sure we are respecting all levels of comfort. If this is how you express and receive appreciation, be mindful that any and all aspects of physical contact must be welcomed and appropriate.*

Begin Here

Appreciation doesn't have to be costly; in fact, it can be as simple as being kind. The most meaningful forms of appreciation often transcend material possessions or extravagant gestures.

Begin by giving your time, energy, and presence to your employees. Actions and encouraging words can go a long way in expressing appreciation.

As you build a culture of appreciation, consider what aligns best with your organization's values and dynamics. It's essential to start with simple and small gestures, and gradually expand from there.

Recap:

- Appreciation outweighs engagement and serves as the foundation for productivity and innovation.
- The cycle of appreciation, feedback, emotional commitment, and engagement is crucial in creating a thriving work environment.
- Genuine appreciation is often overlooked in the workplace, impacting employee engagement and resistance to positive changes.
- There are five appreciation languages: Words, Time, Gifts, Service, and Touch.
- Demonstrating appreciation through kindness, actions, and encouraging words can have a significant impact on employees.

Reflective Question

How can I incorporate the five appreciation languages into my leadership style to better connect with my team?

Action

Find out my appreciation language and those on my direct team.

For further insights on cultivating a culture of appreciation, I recommend checking out Dr. Gary Chapman's insightful books and valuable resources.

"The journey of a thousand miles begins with one step."

Lao Tzu

My journey of homelessness in the workplace began to shift when I finally got the keys to my own apartment within transitional housing. Despite still being in the shelter system and working with a case manager, having a curfew, and certain time restrictions, I started to feel a sense of normalcy.

As my due date approached, I continued to support the oncology department, and just before my leave, I helped bring on a wonderful leave replacement. One of the highlights that will forever stay with me was receiving a call from my case manager informing me that I had been selected for a housing sponsorship by the organization running the shelters. They had reviewed cases, and a house owned by a partnering church had become available.

It was a beautiful 3-bedroom, 2-bath home in a great neighborhood, and they would cover 70% of the rent for a whole year. I qualified for the house based on my case, but I still had to interview with the non-profit board.

The interview room felt like it went on forever, with a table to match. All eyes were on me, and it felt like a hundred people were focused on my every word. As I waddled to the table, I could feel my baby kicking and turning; I was sure this little one felt my nerves. The board wanted to hear my story, my goals, and why I would be the right for this house.

I shared much of the same story I've shared with you—about being homeless, working hard to get hired at five months pregnant, and pushing forward despite the challenges.

I felt warm, shaky, and as if I were in a tunnel. The questions came, and I did my best to answer each one thoughtfully. Though I can't recall all that was said, I'll never forget the energy and vibe in the room.

After the interview, I returned to work, feeling both excited and nervous. A few days later, my case manager called to deliver the news—the board had approved me for the house. I was eight and a half months pregnant, and the timing seemed miraculously aligned.

After work that day, I drove past the house, took a picture, and posted it on Facebook. I finally had a place to bring my baby and my boys. I had a home.

Marlee Nariah Fontes was born on August 17th (the official release date of this book). We named her after the late Bob Marley as she is true representation of One Love. She was sweet, calm, and brought a sense of simplicity to my life during those challenging times.

Once my six-week leave was over, I returned to work to finish out my contract. Unfortunately, due to corporate rules, my contract couldn't be renewed, and my time there came to an end.

My final weeks supporting Valerie were bittersweet. In one of our last meetings, she imparted advice that has stayed with me ever since: "Find a job that fits you and allows you to do what you love."

And so, my journey continued. I eventually left that wonderful little house and embarked on one of the scariest milestones—getting a place of my own. There is so much more to share about this ongoing journey, but that will be for another time.

Valerie the best manager I ever had introduced me to something that has been a driving and grounding force in all I do: Humanity in the Workplace.

As I wrap up this book, I want to share a philosophy that will ground, nourish, and tie together all the chapters in this book.

My story isn't over, nor is it uncommon—humanity is the key to it all.

"Despite all our achievements, we owe our existence to a six-inch layer of topsoil and the fact that it rains."

Unknown

CHAPTER 8

HUMANITY IN THE WORKPLACE

The philosophy of humanity in the workplace centers on recognizing and embracing our shared humanity, which encompasses both our strengths and vulnerabilities. It encourages us to consciously tap into the better parts of our human nature, such as kindness, compassion, understanding, self-reflection, and self-actualization.

By prioritizing these positive aspects of our humanity, we create a workplace environment that is supportive, and inclusive. Kindness and compassion lead to stronger connections between colleagues, fostering understanding, and empathy within the organization.

When we engage in self-reflection and self-actualization, we become more aware of our actions, motivations, and impact on others. This heightened self-awareness enables us to make conscious choices that uplift and empower those around us.

The ripple effect of practicing the best parts of our humanity in the workplace is profound. As employees experience kindness, understanding, and support, they are inspired to reciprocate and extend the same attitude to their colleagues. This creates a positive feedback loop that not only elevates the workplace culture but also extends beyond the office environment.

The transformational power of humanity in the workplace goes beyond the professional realm and permeates into our homes, communities, and society at large. When humans are treated like humans in the workplace, they carry that experience into their personal lives. It shapes the way they interact with family, friends, and community.

In essence, humanity in the workplace is a catalyst for a broader cultural shift. It prompts us to consider the impact of our actions and words on others, encouraging a more compassionate and understanding society. By fostering an environment where the best parts of our humanity are celebrated, we create a world that is more empathetic, supportive, and conducive to positive change.

Embracing humanity in the workplace is not just a professional approach; it is a way of life that has the potential to transform individuals, organizations, and the world at large. It is a philosophy that reminds us of our shared humanity and empowers us to lead with kindness, compassion, and a genuine desire to uplift and influence others positively.

Ubuntu

Ubuntu is an African philosophy that means "I am because we are," or my humanness is tied to your humanness.

Nelson Mandela and Desmond Tutu embraced the philosophy of Ubuntu in their efforts to unify South Africa following the end of South African apartheid. What Ubuntu represented was instrumental in fostering reconciliation and building a new, inclusive national identity.

Embracing the Ubuntu philosophy with Humanity in the Workplace translates the values of interconnectedness, empathy, and mutual respect from a societal context into an organizational one. Here's what that means for the workplace:

Interconnected Success: Embracing Ubuntu means recognizing that individual success is tied to the success of the team and the organization. Employees work collaboratively, understanding that their well-being and achievements are interlinked. It fosters a culture where accomplishments are celebrated collectively.

Empathy and Understanding: Ubuntu encourages a compassionate approach where colleagues seek to understand each other's perspectives, strengths, and vulnerabilities. This create a supportive environment, reducing conflict and fostering positive relationships.

Inclusivity: Ubuntu played a role in fostering reconciliation and unity in South Africa, it can help create an inclusive workplace. By recognizing the shared humanity in all employees, regardless of their background, Ubuntu promotes a culture where everyone feels valued and included.

Responsibility and Accountability: In an Ubuntu-infused workplace, individuals feel a heightened sense of responsibility towards their colleagues and the wider organization. This can lead to increased accountability, ethical behavior, and integrity in daily operations.

Enhanced Collaboration: Ubuntu fosters a spirit of collaboration, with employees working together towards common goals rather than competing against one another. This teamwork can lead to more creative problem-solving and greater overall productivity.

Ripple Effects Beyond the Workplace: Ubuntu principles helped heal and unite a nation, they can have positive ripple effects beyond the workplace. Employees who experience a culture infused with Ubuntu may carry those values into their personal lives, strengthening family and community relationships.

Healing: Ubuntu's emphasis on forgiveness and reconciliation can provide a framework for handling workplace conflicts and setbacks. This can lead to healing which helps teams come back stronger from challenges.

Humanity in the Workplace and Ubuntu are solid ways organizations can build strong, unified teams and foster a culture that's good for business and contributes positively to society at large.

This is where we start.

CLOSURE

In many ways, I feel like this book could have been two pages that would read; **Tame the ego. Raise the humanity.**

However, speaking directly to the ego wouldn't yield the same transformative journey as highlighting the things the ego directly affects.

The main reason company cultures go to shit is because the ego is making decisions that conflict with the essence of our humanity.

The shitty feelings, experiences, and outcomes are all symptoms of that.

The ego reacts. Humanity responds.

The ego is your false self that believes in its separation and always strives to acquire and achieve. It's constantly in search of more. Your ego can't coexist with awareness and alignment; it can't survive in the now. The ego is always trying to keep you in the past or future.

This behavior causes conflict with the better parts of humanity and directly impacts others.

So while grand statements, strategies, and initiatives are great if ego is the driver, your culture and business will go to shit and take you along with it.

How Do You Keep Your Company Culture From Going To Shit?

- Understand the Origin and Energy of the Workplace
- Transcend Traditional Human Resources
- Remove Deep Fake Perks
- Seek Culture Adds
- Design a Meaningful Welcome & Onboarding
- Lead from a Place Beyond Yourself
- Diversify the Way You Show Appreciation
- Embrace Humanity and Ubuntu in the Workplace

It's not a hard problem; it's a heart problem.

So with that, I encourage you to:
Tame the ego. Raise the humanity.

If you'd like to learn more about company culture or are interested in partnering with Culture Circle to enrich your organization's culture, visit culturecircle.co.

"I was once asked why I don't participate in anti-war demonstrations. I said that I would never do that, but as soon as you have a pro-peace rally, I'll be there."

Mother Teresa

CHAPTER 9

BONUS DUMP

This compilation consists of various topics I've written and thought about related or unrelated to company culture in particular order or form.

The Sphincters

We have multiple sphincters within our bodies.

What is fascinating about the sphincter is that it controls some critical functions of the human body, such as breathing, speaking, pooping, urinating, digesting, and giving birth.

The sphincter operates best when we feel safe and relaxed.

So, imagine with me for a second that a woman is giving birth in a cave back in the caveman days, and a saber-toothed tiger comes up - the sphincter would shut, and the woman would be able to pick up and birth her baby somewhere else. In most vaginal births, when the cervix isn't dilating or effacing, the sphincter-like mechanism is the cause.

Let's move on to poop.

Because of the instinctual mechanism, your body won't poop unless it feels safe or relaxed. The survival purpose is that when you poop, you are in a vulnerable position, and if there were a predator nearby, you most likely wouldn't survive. So, we are wired to poop when it is safe—also part of the sphincter's mechanism.

Now, what does this have to do with culture and business?

A lot.

The other thing that the sphincter controls is how and when we speak up, and similar to birth or taking a poop, the sphincter will close shut when there is a threat or it doesn't feel safe.

It also controls the breath - which has been tied to how we mitigate stress, regulate blood pressure and receive oxygen to the brain.

This is very important as we navigate the workplace.

So, if you have a toxic or unhealthy workplace where fear is one of the core mechanisms within the culture, you won't have a culture that speaks up and contributes ideas.

And if people do speak up, their ideas will lack creativity because when there is a perceived threat, cortisol is released. Cortisol numbs creativity, innovation, game-changing ideas, and breakthroughs.

Plus, the culture collectively can sense when this is happening, which flows into not feeling like their work has meaning, or they start to question their purpose. In theory, they know that possibilities aren't reaching their full potential because of this dynamic.

Most workplaces are multidimensional and multigenerational, and the ideas within could solve and contribute some dynamic shifts for a company and beyond if allowed.

The shift towards seeking culture add rather than culture fit transforms the workplace.

So, the next time you think about your culture and work environment, ask yourself: Are my people birthing, creating new things, speaking up and sharing ideas, and pooping (the ability to release waste and what doesn't belong)? Because if they can, you have a culture that will transform and evolve beyond what you can imagine.

When Companies Say "We're a Family"

Employees don't want to be "a family". They want to be treated with humanity and when they signed their offer letter, they didn't sign up for:

- Microaggression
- Discrimination
- Negitive Politics
- Disrespect
- Being Yelled At
- Name-calling
- Lack of direction
- Deep Fake Perks
- Sexual Harassment
- Racism
- Ageism
- Sexism
- Ableism
- Gossip
- Poor leadership
- Lack of constructive feedback

Miss them with all that and create a culture that amplifies the best parts of humanity.

Values

Not done properly.

Not practiced.

Lack of purpose or meaning.

These are the top reasons why a company's values fail.

When I collaborate with companies to create or refine their values, I consistently provide the following guidance:

No More Than 3-5 Values: Think of values like kids; the more you have, the harder it becomes to recall each one's details. Embracing 3-5 core values strikes a balance that ensures your people remember and consistently practice them throughout the organization.

Practicable Inside and Outside the Workplace: Values should make sense beyond the workplace's confines. An essential question to ask is: Can our values extend beyond the workplace setting and still carry significance?

Consider a value like "Put the customer first." While meaningful within the office, it should also resonate outside of work. True values are interchangeable.

Internal Systems Must Align with Values: Everything, from initial Hello-to-Hire and everything in between, must align harmoniously with the chosen values. This unity is the bedrock of success.

Clear Definitions for Each Value: Definitions must be simple, easy to remember, and recite. Avoid overly complex interpretations. Values that are hard to define won't remain in people's minds.

Memorability is Key: Everyone, including Leadership, should effortlessly recite the values at any moment, along with being able to tell you what they mean. This underscores why a range of 3-5 values is optimal.

Avoid Vanity Values: Values should radiate meaning rather than flashiness. Focus on their significance and depth rather than making them appear attractive.

Resist Copying Others' Values: Adopting borrowed or copied values leads to conflict. Your culture is distinctive; invest time in discovering what truly aligns. It's okay to draw inspiration from other companies but ensure your values authentically resonate.

Design Values for Longevity: Don't rush the creation process. Crafting values that withstand the test of time requires careful consideration. Once they're firmly established, the momentum will naturally follow.

Hire and Fire Aligned with Values: The values you hold dear should synchronize with every hire and even inform your decisions about personnel changes.

Leadership Must Lead by Example: Upholding values is imperative for leadership. Requesting your team to venture where you're unwilling to go is a classic example of ineffective leadership.

Bonus Tip: As Stan Slap wisely puts it, companies don't possess values; people do.

culture and influence how your company navigates its unique ecosystem. If achieving total alignment is challenging, the cornerstone of kindness and embracing the finest aspects of humanity can serve as a guiding light.

You rarely need values when things are going well.

Be mindful of how you create them; when done right, they yield transcending results.

D.E.I

DEI stands for;
Diversity; a range of different things
Equity; the quality of being fair and impartial.
Inclusion; the action or state of including or being included within a group or structure.

DEI seems like three little letters.
To our brains, easy to say, remember and repeat.

However, similar to texting and driving, which is not safe, our brains also make logical exceptions and rational - we can text, we can drive, we can text and drive.

Yet, there's a problem. While we might feel fully capable of texting and driving based on our brain's rationale, we tend to overlook road conditions and other variables like other drivers. This combination creates a dangerous situation, even though many of us continue to engage in it.

Diversity vs. Selective Diversity

By nature, every human we encounter is diverse - that is an absolute based on the definition of diversity.

Have you ever hired or met someone who wasn't diverse?

Where a lot of companies misstep was focusing on Selective Diversity. Selective diversity is when companies focus only on specific types of diversity.

For example, focusing on hiring more Black people, women, or non-binary is selective diversity..

By doing this, you are being exclusive, not inclusive, and exclusion by inclusion is still exclusion.

Next, we have E-for Equity.

Equity is relative, depending on the lens through which you view it. What most companies are likely trying to accomplish or establish is equality, meaning the state of being equal, especially in status, rights, and opportunities. Equality establishes an absolute foundation, whereas equity relies on individuals or groups adopting a mindset that benefits all, not just some.

Another way I've looked at the word equity is through company shares: everyone gets a different amount based on their role, title, salary, and relationship to the business. If we were to apply equality to the shares scenario, everyone would receive the same amount of shares when they join a company.

Next is inclusion - this is where the money is.

Inclusion is the core of the DEI equation. By focusing on inclusion, diversity is welcomed and has a chance to thrive. Equality paves the way for equity, and everything flows in the path of least resistance.

If the company culture is shit, DEI can't exist.

DEI, built on a broken company culture, will not succeed. Throwing up faux DEI and anti-racist statements won't make this any less true. Companies now see that DEI is the marathon that they didn't prepare or stretch for, nor did the culture have the water it needed to navigate through the training designed to unite, although they were divisive.

Critical thinking, being less reactive, and being more intentional would have helped companies pause and assess what they were doing.

A considerable investment of time, energy, and resources was utilized, leaving an anti-climatic vibe around DEI in the workplace.

It's time to do DEI differently, and addressing why burnout can show us how.

Burnout in D.E.I

Burnout is nature's way of telling us we are on the path of most resistance.

Here are five reasons why burnout is happening in DEI:

#1. The Culture Wasn't Ready

After George Floyd's murder, a good amount of companies adopted or dusted off their DEI efforts in 2020.

During that time, the macro culture (what is happening in the world) influenced the micro-cultures (what was happening in home spaces and workplaces)—creating a shock to most company cultures, who, up until this point, went from rarely uttered the word racism to it brought up in every Zoom call—paired with a pandemic where lives and livelihoods were in the balance. Workplace cultures went into full protective mode.

Building anything significant in an unhealthy workplace culture is a poor use of energy, time, and money. The culture will reject it, and it will be a one-hit-wonder of initiatives that the culture won't forget.

Knowing where your culture is makes a huge difference.

Cultures need to be primed and ready to receive anything new; in this case, something new was initiatives that seemed simple but carried more weight than expected.

When companies began scrambling to launch DEI initiatives, most didn't have a budget, plan, or any idea where to start—hiring the first experts they Googled and went to work building complex systems on a broken foundation.

The culture wasn't ready -the foundation needed repair. On top of that, companies had no business putting out anti-racism statements while their own people were dealing with oppressing behaviors in the workplace.

Mix that with no budget and disengaged leadership; DEI never had a chance. Not even with the right people doing the work.

#2. The Language

Our words carry energy, and we carry energy in our words. That energy is equal to mass, momentum, and manifestation. It materializes into existence.

Using disempowering language takes a toll on you in ways you don't recognize.

Using words like anti-racism, minorities, white supremacy, privilege, marginalized, POC, BIPOC, and diversity in the context of a specific type of person's visual identity.

Another way to simplify this concept is: to imagine waking up each morning and telling yourself how horrible, ugly, and worthless you are. Do you think you will have a great day or quality of life?

Yet, we are doing the same thing around a topic and area we are looking to invoke positive change, transformation, and impact.

It's not working because the words "anti-racism" is low vibrational. They psychologically do not help us overcome the issues of racism because white supremacy, privilege, minority, and marginalized are all low vibrational and require a different approach.

If you're trying to solve something that is already low vibe, you don't go any lower because it's going to exhaust you.

And you can't solve or grow past something by using the same energy to create it.

For example, if you are using the word "minorities" in your work, consider the energy around that word and reflect on if it is empowering or not.

When our words shift, change happens. The trajectory of that change depends on the vibration of our words.

For the record and I might be the only one but I have never referred to myself as a POC or BIPOC, nor did I hear this language until 2020, but this is for a whole other subject, but I feel such words put a further divide and later when it comes to our humanity.

#3. Company Guilt

As I mentioned earlier, DEI amplified after the murder of George Floyd.

While consulting with a company on their workplace culture, I joined their DEI channel on Slack and noticed that from May to July 2020, it was full of comments, articles, quotes, and insights. I asked the CEO why the activity stopped. He said very candidly; it's no longer in the news.

Whenever something is done or created due to guilt or fear, those emotions become woven into its fabric, affecting everything it produces, and whatever is produced is short-lived and lacks lasting impact.

DEI created out of a company's reactive nature or guilt isn't going to have the same outcome as DEI created out of a thoughtful, conscious reflection of the need and the why behind it.

#4. Unrealistic Expectations

Expectations become exhausting when they are unachievable. It's like spinning wheels and not going anywhere.

Critical thinking is critical when setting DEI expectations.

For example, setting a goal to see and hire candidates of a specific ethnicity goes against the grain of inclusion.

Exclusion by inclusion is still exclusion.

Not having a budget or resources to do the DEI job properly is not only a setup for failure; it's unrealistic. As I've shared previously, DEI is deeper than most anticipate - those three little letters add up.

One of the most significant unrealistic expectations leading to burnout is timing. Most people who bring in someone to lead DEI efforts expect change to happen as soon as the ink dries. Change takes time.

Humanity and things tied to it can't be automatically downloaded or on demand. It takes time, and just because there is a fire under these initiatives, you have to pace it so it doesn't burn and go to ash.

Conversations about expectations paired with critical thinking and humanity go a long way.

My advice is to start simple and start small. Great things take time, and if you want your DEI to be great, be prepared for it to take time.

#5. Telling the story from the wound instead of the scar

Some parts of this work will wound you or open up old wounds, so continuous proactive healing is needed.

As a birth doula, I have seen many births go to plan, some not, and some that took a huge toll physically and emotionally. With each one, I cry to release as it brings up something in me. Very early on, I learned that rituals help me heal to carry fresh energy into the birthing space. But even before that, I had to heal from my birth experiences. None of them were terrible experiences, but in the event, I suppressed something that could come out in my work or interaction with a family, I had to heal it all.

Each experience you don't heal from is carried into the work. It is a wound that hasn't healed.

Examples of telling the story from the wound manifest into telling people to "Be Less White," to recognize their privilege, or calling out a specific demographic of people based not on their character but by the color of their skin - none of this is empowering.

Burnout will only amplify the lowest vibration within.

It's okay to acknowledge you are still healing in the area others are looking for guidance in. Remember to tell stories from the scar once they are healed, not from the wound.

So if you are looking to do DEI differently, reverse these points of burnout:

- Tell the story from the scar vs. the wound. You need facilitators who are transformational in their approach and ability to guide others to better.
- Set realistic expectations: timing, budget, focus, goals
- Release guilt: it will not serve you in the space you wish to impact true change and transformation
- Use high vibrational language: our words have power and carry a frequency. We can't solve the problem with the same energy or words used to create it.
- Prepare the culture: do the culture work first.

Why Being Anti-Racism Company Won't End Racism

When I heard companies committing to being anti-racist organizations, I knew things would get interesting.

I get the intent.

We want to be a company or organization that is actively ending racism (*the belief that one ethnicity is inferior or superior to another*) inside and outside the workplace.

And if that is true, the statement of anti-racism isn't the right word to use.

I speak about this more in-depth in an article called Be Less White - inspired by a leading soda company in the U.S.

Many companies focus their anti-racist education and actions on calling out white employees, white people and highlighting Black trauma.

If no one has said this — that isn't how to end racism.

Something is off if we are condemning and guilting each other, perpetuating more of what we don't want to see. There is more understanding that needs to happen. It goes beyond donating and taking training that condemns or calls out a specific ethnicity or demographic.

Companies committing to being anti-racist happened so quickly that they missed critical thinking and asking the right questions.

I teach a workshop called *How to Become A Racist*; over 100 participants have answered the million-dollar question: How do you become racist?

Not one answer says by not donating or not hiring Black people. Yet, that is what many companies committed to in 2020.

Racism is a heart problem.
Not a hard problem.

Money can solve most hard problems - it can't solve what is enclosed in the heart.

If companies are serious about this work, they will re-evaluate the company culture and foundational parts of the business.

The truth is if you become focused on DEI, anti-racism, or hiring "more Black people" after George Floyd was killed, there is a big chance you have done it wrong, upset a few people, and wasted valuable resources.

Companies will need to restart and rephrase the language they have been using if they wish to see change.

Racism is not a Black and White issue. It's a Humanity issue.

Racism is oppressive. If there are other forms of oppression within the workplace, how can you effectively address racism?

And since racism, sexism, ageism, ableism, colorism, and classism carry the same vibration - if companies don't use a different approach, these other 'isms will continue.

Companies: Fix your internal oppression first.

When employees are afraid to speak up, that is oppression.

When employees are being yelled at in the workplace, that is oppression.

When someone is bullied in the workplace, that is oppression.

When employees are treated wrong, that is oppression.

When employees are overworked, that is oppression.

When employees are underpaid. That. Is. Oppression.

Stop the performance. We need authentic companies.

We need more companies willing to do what most won't.

We need companies that don't follow the in-trends because everyone else is doing it.

We need companies that dare to be the Miles Davis, Michelangelo, and Rosa Parks of the world.

We need companies that recognize that traditional business won't outlive humanity.

We need companies to honor the humans they have, and by doing so, they create environments of empowerment, and those empowered humans will go out into the world and assist in the change in the world.

We need companies that will dance first. Not follow the next sheep off a cliff.

"And those who were seen dancing were thought to be insane by those who could not hear the music."— Friedrich Nietzsche

Racism is an antiquated problem.

We are one race with a blend of beautiful ethnicities that have come here for a purpose. Our words have cut out and brought humanity down for so long - suffocating progress and disempowering solutions.

If you are a company that wants to have a positive impact on ending racism - use words and actions that transcend beyond the basic narrative.

Start with doing the internal work that will be the light that will shine from your organization.

Racism has been a part of our humanity for a long time, thus requiring a different approach that goes beyond isolating two or three ethnicities to solve it.

There is simplicity in ending racism; however, there is a balance of complexity in the simplicity, and the complexity is rooted in our society that often does not go quietly.

Companies need to rethink the words they are using to actively end racism inside and outside of the workplace.

Ubuntu (I am because we are).

Live Long and Prosper

I often draw inspiration from Star Trek when designing my workshops. Ever since I was a child, I have been captivated by the vast universe and diverse races that inhabit the space vessels in the show. As an adult, I've come to appreciate the profound lessons that can be applied to our daily lives.

One character that stands out is Spock, who was both revered and disliked. Initially, people were put off by his appearance without considering the qualities he represented. This reminds me of the insightful quote by Soren Kierkegaard: "Life can only be understood backward, but it must be lived forwards." Despite the initial resistance, Spock became one of the most influential characters in the entire Star Trek series.

What fascinated me about Spock was his struggle to reconcile his Vulcan and human sides. This internal battle mirrors the conflicts we face in many aspects of our lives, particularly when it comes to our humanity. We all possess higher and lower versions of ourselves, and how we choose to show up depends on which side we embrace and align with.

In all that I have shared and learned so far, I have a knowingness that our choices regarding our humanity extend far beyond our imagination. We all yearn for a fulfilling life, one in which we can Live Long and Prosper.

BIRTHING THIS BOOK

Holy shit, I did it.

I've written the book that's been inside me since my homeless experience. 'How to Keep Your Company Culture From Going to Shit' began as five orange, poorly formatted slides, with a few topics I started connecting to company culture.

I never considered myself a writer; in fact, I was embarrassed about my writing and would avoid it at all costs. A severe concussion I suffered when I was younger changed how I perceive and process words.

So when I say 'holy shit,' I mean it with everything.

This book wasn't written traditionally; during the writing of this book, I had two home births and one very dark postpartum. I've written parts of this book at 2 am and late at night when all the kids are asleep after a full day. I captured random, inspired thoughts as I rushed out of the shower to grab a nearby recorder, all while taming my ego and its narrative that nobody would want to read what I had to say.

Writing this book has been like another pregnancy and labor.

Much like the birth of my little humans, I am the facilitator of this book's journey. I relinquish control and yield to the universe, letting it decide where and what parts of this book land.

As I wrote, I stayed focused on my vision of creating a visually captivating coffee-table book that anyone could pick up, diving into various topics that impact workplace culture and humanity.

If you are thinking of writing a book, do it.

Don't get stuck on how it will get done; start writing.

If your hand gets tired, outline the subject and core topics, then speak into a recorder and transcribe your words. If the words won't flow, put on your favorite song and sing out loud or take a nap. Don't force flow.

I have a saying for giving birth and in life: If you're not 10 centimeters, don't push.

Just know you've got this.

As I close out this book, I'm in my room with fairy lights illuminating my space and soothing, high-vibrational music playing in the background.

It humbles me that you're reading these words right now. I send you light and love for your journey as you navigate your humanity; I hope you release the stories that no longer serve you, find what lights you up, and make your heart sing. May peace find you inside and outside the workplace, and may abundance and prosperity seek and find you.

Thank you for reading my book and witnessing this birth.

It's important to share that this is my second attempt at this book.

The first book was a blend of spontaneous creativity and forced effort. Due to my still-undefined writing style, I have yet to actively promote it. However, this book mirrors more of my present self as I continue to learn and evolve.

This book's intention differs from my previous work. I aimed to unveil the intricate workings of my mind, what my heart perceives in the ecosystem, and the profound insights I hold. Instead of relying solely on heavy research or providing step-by-step instructions, I ventured into philosophy. I explored my ideas concerning humanity in the workplace and its connection with company culture.

I wanted to offer more of myself instead of adhering to a rigid framework or a linear sequence of ideas. If your heart harbors a message yearning to be expressed, you should pursue it without waiting for all the puzzle pieces to fall perfectly into place. Because the truth is, they never will. Trust your intuition and allow your creative energy to flow naturally.

I often think of the wisdom shared by Bruce Lee and Lao Tzu about being like water – a beautiful concept that resonates deeply.

My aspiration is that you enjoyed reading this book and that it sparked at least one idea for you, whether it pertains to the workplace or your personal life. Regardless of where your opinions align, I warmly invite you to connect with me, as I welcome genuine human connections on a deeper level.

All that said, book number two might be coming soon.

Pun intended.

Light and love to you,

Charisse

"Nothing in the world is as soft and yielding as water. Yet for dissolving the hard and inflexible, nothing can surpass it."

Lao Tzu, Tao Te Ching – Verse 78

"Be water, my friend."

Bruce Lee

GRATITUDE

My heart is filled with gratitude for the support, guidance, and love I received when writing this book.

To my husband, this is baby number seven. Thank you.
To my kids, you truly inspire me; thank you for choosing me.
To my parents, if y'all made it this far, thank you.
A mi suegra. Te amo.
To Barbara, thank you for being my mentor and friend.
To Andrea, I pushed.
To Kelsey, hands up!
To Maria, fainting gif:
To Luisa, party parrot:
To Alyssa, Namaste,
To the best manager, I ever had, thank you beyond words.
To the recruiter that found me, I am grateful.
Thank you to every client partner that welcomed me into your space, allowing me to do the woo and the work.

To you reading this right now, thank you, I am grateful.

To me: WOW!

You've come to the end, which is also the beginning of something. Thank you for taking the time and energy to read my book. I am grateful and hope that it has added something to assist you along your journey.

If you'd like to go deeper into anything shared in this book, please visit culturecircle.co/shit and enjoy tons of free resources and content related to culture.

Vibe with this book?
Let's connect on Linkedin: Charisse Fontes
Share this book with someone
Write a review of Gratitude
Send me an email: charisse@culturecircle.co
Visit: culturecircle.co
Write me a letter:
Charisse Fontes
4425-C Treat Blvd #333
Concord, CA 94521

ABOUT THE AUTHOR

Charisse Fontes likes to share that she is human first. With her humanness, she is an author, international speaker, and visionary thought leader in the culture industry, where she dedicates her career to exploring the dimensions of culture, humanity, and personal growth.

As the Founder of Culture Circle, a boutique culture partner that creates healthy and inclusive workplaces for culture-conscious companies and has held pivotal leadership roles across various industries, Charisse continuously breaks new ground. Her transcending approach to organizational culture and operations stands as a testament to her leadership.

Charisse is an anthropologist and birth doula, which offers a uniquely human-centered approach to her work, solidifying her reputation as a trusted advisor and strategic leader in the field. Beyond the corporate realm, she's channeled her passion for humanity into leading an educational non-profit. This initiative aims to guide humanity within communities to end harmful 'isms.'

Born and raised in the Bay Area, California, Charisse lives with her husband, six kids, and an abundance of plants. She is also a Trekkie, part-time DJ, intuitive guide, angler, and a student of meditation.

To connect or work with Charisse, visit:

Linkedin: Charisse Fontes
Culture Circle: culturecircle.co
charissefontes.com

My epitaph:

Charisse Alayna Fontes | Human

She did what made her heart sing and did it for the audience of One.

Made in the USA
Las Vegas, NV
01 October 2024

96101265R00095